PROFESSIONAL PERSPECTIVE DRAWING
FOR ARCHITECTS
AND ENGINEERS

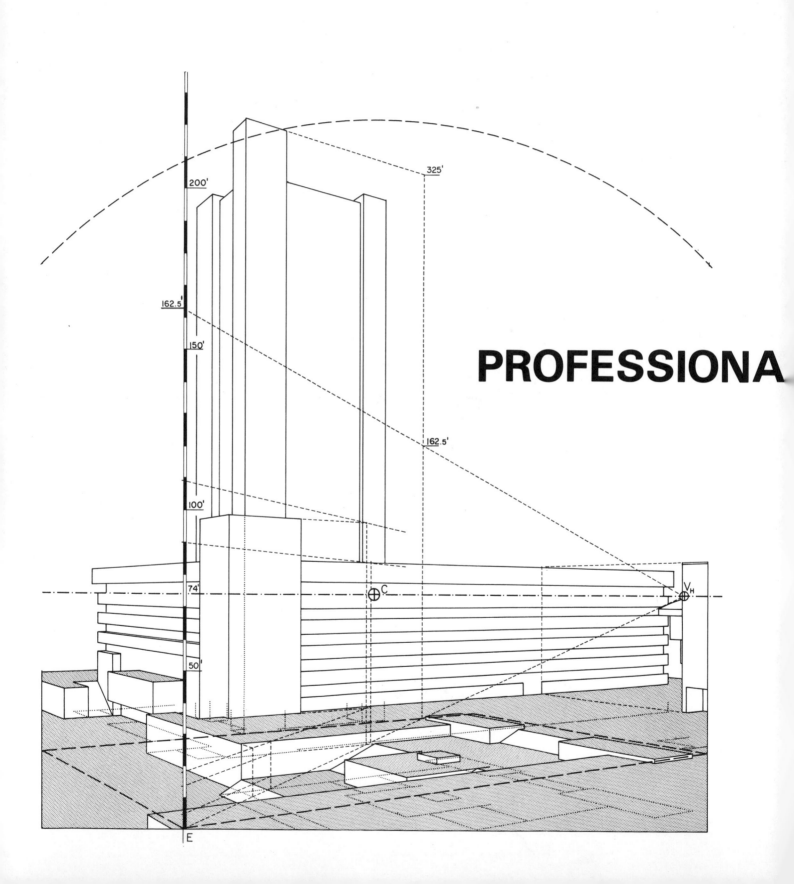

PROFESSIONA

PERSPECTIVE DRAWING FOR ARCHITECTS AND ENGINEERS

Friedrich W. Capelle

McGRAW-HILL BOOK COMPANY

New York   St. Louis   San Francisco   London   Sydney
Toronto   Mexico   Panama

PROFESSIONAL PERSPECTIVE DRAWING
FOR ARCHITECTS AND ENGINEERS

Copyright © 1969 by McGraw-Hill, Inc. All Rights Reserved.
Printed in the United States of America. No part of this
publication may be reproduced, stored in a retrieval system,
or transmitted, in any form or by any means, electronic,
mechanical, photocopying, recording, or otherwise, without
the prior written permission of the publisher.
Library of Congress Catalog Card Number 69–12407

ISBN 07-009776-3

4567890 HDBP 765

To Ruth Ordelheide Capelle

PREFACE

"Professional Perspective Drawing for Architects and Engineers" is the result of the author's many years of experience in the field of architecture. The book comes from the drawing board and is designed to be used with it. It offers to the designer and to the student clear rules and guidelines which allow the construction of accurate, aesthetically satisfactory perspectives substantially faster than the conventional methods.

Normal approach to viewing pictures is an essential part of the construction of a true perspective. The observer's distance from the object, determined by the common angle of sight, and the object's displacement to the picture plane are related to the size of the available drawing board. This relationship can be expressed by *formulas* in order to find the size and correct location of the perspective between the vanishing points. The book thus reverses the conventional method by enabling the designer to start with the determination of the size of the perspective and then derive the location of the vanishing points, which in return are related to the size of the available drawing board. The most preferable view can be selected from the outset.

The basic procedure always starts with the selection of an *auxiliary rectangle, which should frame the most interesting area.* The construction of the perspective proceeds from this rectangle; it can thus be regarded as the core of the future picture. Should it not comply with the anticipated picture, the designer can abandon it at this early stage without having wasted time.

Contrary to all theories and methods taught at architectural schools or presented in literature on perspective drawing, most of which restrict themselves to the 45° perspective, this book consists of ten different perspectives.

These perspectives are demonstrated with the same object as seen from different station points, thus clearly indicating the substantial advantages of one over the other, depending on the individual purpose of the presentation. The designer chooses the one which comes closest to his image. He then simply follows the instructions for that method.

The guesswork, the uncertainty about the outcome, and the unpleasant distortions have been eliminated. Consequently, the wide-angle perspective with its inevitable distortions will not be discussed.

Yet the *high-rising buildings* of our time fall far beyond the circle of undistorted projection. To capture them in true perspective and develop the picture to its maximum extent from the drawing board, a *specific formula* for the P_H *projection* has been introduced. Each instruction contains an analysis regarding the height of the object.

The rendering of a perspective construction is an entirely different matter and already well covered by other publications. It is an art. To construct a perspective, however, is a skill, acquirable and learnable by everyone. Therefore, the gifted renderer, too, should use this book, because it gives him the true facts to begin with.

It is hoped that this book closes a gap and opens a new chapter on constructing perspectives accurately and quickly.

The author's most sincere gratitude goes to the late Professor Dr. Georg Scheffer. He introduced his students at the Technische Universität Berlin, the former T.H. in Berlin-Charlottenburg, to geometry and perspectives profoundly and imaginatively, so that these studies never ceased to intrigue my mind. He laid the groundwork from which I could proceed to my own findings.

Among my colleagues it was William F. Doemland, Architect, who kept urging me to publish the methods which he had seen in practice. I deeply appreciate his professional recognition.

The amount of encouragement and understanding which my wife has given me and her help in organizing and programming the material and typing the manuscript have made this book a part of her own.

Friedrich W. Capelle

CONTENTS

chapter one

PERSPECTIVES WITH COMMON EYE LEVEL

INTRODUCTION

A Chinese philosopher once said, "Even a journey of a thousand miles has to begin with a first single step." In drawing a perspective, this first step is to position the vertical center line of the perspective in the correct place between the major vanishing points on the mathematical horizon. If this is done superficially, the designer later has to deal with distortions, which are time-consuming, cumbersome, and unpleasant to retouch. This approach is also uneconomical, because the hours of painstaking corrections could have been spent more creatively to bring life and scale to the illustration.

There are three causes of distortion to be avoided: (1) the view of a perspective from a wrong station point; (2) the incorrect projection of the object upon the picture plane; and (3) the projection from an uncommon station point by exceeding the angle of sight. These three causes will not be detailed, since the purpose of the book is to give instructions for the right and fast way of doing a perspective projection by eliminating the most obvious and disturbing distortions.

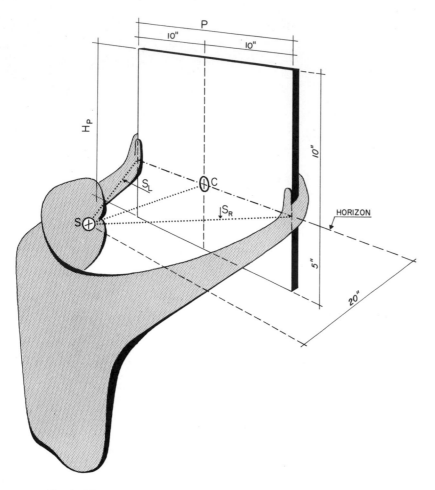

Fig. 1, 0-1

    This drawing shows the normal condition under which a man views a rendering of common and suitable size, 20 × 15 in. As shown on the diagram, the mathematical horizon of the perspective is at eye level, and the central line of sight SC penetrates the picture at the center C of the perspective, which is not its center of gravity. C is not only the intersection of the bisecting vertical center line and the horizon, but also the projection of the station point S at the right angle on the horizon. The indicated dimensions—the distance from the station point to the center of the picture $SC = 20$ in., the width of the picture $P = 20$ in., the height of the picture $H_p = 15$ in., and the horizon measured at 5 in. from the groundline of the picture—are based on the experience that an observer looks at a picture from a distance approximately equal to its width. The larger the picture, the farther an observer will unconsciously step back in order to get an undistorted impression of it. This unconscious tendency is generally not noticed by the unexperienced designer; many renderings are distorted since they are not observed from the proper station point.

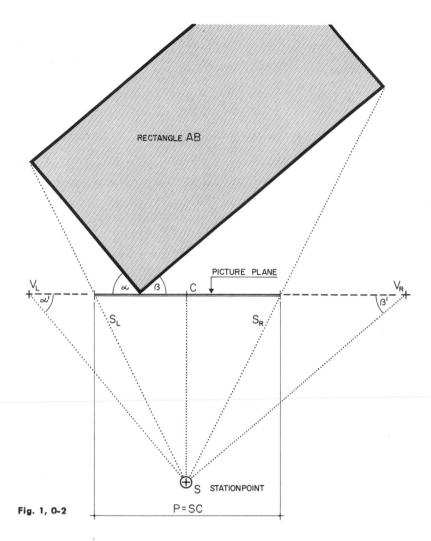

RECTANGLE AB

PICTURE PLANE

V_L α β C

α' S_L S_R β' V_R

$\oplus S$ STATIONPOINT

Fig. 1, 0-2 $P = SC$

Where is the station point to be?   It should be opposite the center of the picture at eye level at a distance equal at least to the width of the rendering. This rule is employed as the leading principle throughout this book.

Figure 1, 0-2* is constructed according to this rule.   It shows the proper location of the station point S in relation to the center of the picture, the object AB, and the two vanishing points V_L and V_R.   Since we have learned by experience that SC should not be less than the width of the picture P, SC is a function of P; i.e., SC increases or decreases at the same ratio as P. By the same token we have to realize that T, the distance from the left vanishing point V_L to the right vanishing point V_R, is a function of SC.   Each change of SC will affect the size of T according to the trigonometrical formula $T = (\tan \alpha' + \tan \beta')\, SC$, on the basis that $\alpha + \beta = 90°$, $\alpha = \alpha'$, $\beta = \beta'$.

T is also affected if the angles of position of the object change, but SC stays unchanged.   In other words, these three factors T, SC, and the position of the object determined by the angles α and β are correlated.

*Figure designations should be read as follows: In Fig. 1, 2-5, for example, 1 represents Chapter 1, 2 represents Method 2, and 5 represents Illustration 5.

The size of the object does not influence the size of the perspective, the distance between the vanishing points, or the distance from the station point to the picture plane. A skyscraper can be captured in a 35-mm slide and a bacteria shown upon a movie screen. The size of the object is relative or undefinable unless properly related to human size in the rendering.

To the designer, bound to the limits of his tools, the most determinant of these factors is T, the distance between vanishing points, because it is limited by the width of the drawing board. The size of a rendering cannot be set accurately without taking this factor into account. It is difficult and time-consuming to work with a vanishing point located beyond the table. Therefore, each description of a case presented in this book will be preceded by a formula which will enable the designer to find the maximum size of the rendering quickly according to the available drawing board. Then he chooses the angle of the object's position to the picture plane and derives the measurements of his intended perspective. The designer will thus be assured that the distortions on the vertical and horizontal planes of the object have been eliminated, as long as the height and width of the perspective do not go beyond the circle of undistorted projection, as illustrated in Fig. 1, 0-3.

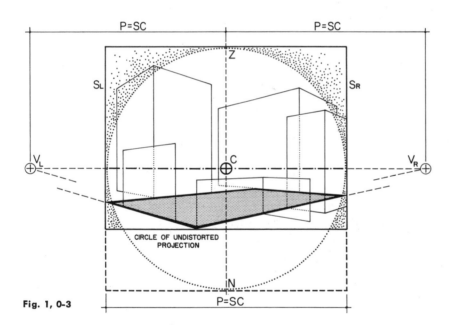

Fig. 1, 0-3

The center of this circle coincides with the center C of the perspective, and its diameter is equal to the distance SC. The areas beyond the circle are in the range of obvious distortion. As the picture is laid out, the upper areas beyond the perimeter are larger than the rather insignificant ones below the horizon. This is caused by the low horizon to which all horizontal lines of the object converge. When the horizon is raised, the distorted areas below the horizon increase as the upper distorted areas decrease. The picture may become unsatisfactory if not unpleasant. Men are more aware of anomalies below than above eye level.

A perfect solution would be a square in a circle, but that is not the ideal shape of a picture. However, the method is more flexible. Should the height of the object exceed its diagonal width, then the distance of the vanishing points and the diameter of the circle of undistorted projection will be determined by the height of the object. In any case, the distance from vanishing point to vanishing point, the location of the center of the perspective on the horizon, and the circle of undistorted projection are the determinant factors for the size of the perspective.

Hence, it can be stated that obvious distortions will be eliminated by determining the width and the height of the perspective in accordance with the circle of undistorted projection.

The height of the horizon as one-fourth of SC measured from the ground-line of the perspective is desirable, although not always appropriate.

As a rule of practice, it is recommended that the designer construct a perspective in the range of 30×20 in. at a drawing board of about 5 ft. Larger perspectives can be attained by photographic means. The size of a perspective, however, should not be less than 12×8 in. Six inches is the minimum distance for the human eye to focus upon.

METHOD 1:   Central Perspective

Characteristics

One side of the rectangle *AB* is the picture plane. This perspective has one vanishing point *C* in the center of the picture plane at the horizon.

The maximal width P_{max} of the perspective equals the distance *SC* from the station point *S* to the center *C* of the perspective; i.e.,

$$P_{max} = SC$$

It should not exceed 30 in.

The height H_o of the object at its intersection with the picture plane has to be equal to or less than $\frac{3}{4}P_{max}$; i.e.,

$$H_o \leq \frac{3}{4}P_{max}$$

Applicability

Perspectives of streets, malls, corridors, plazas, halls, bridges, and the like.

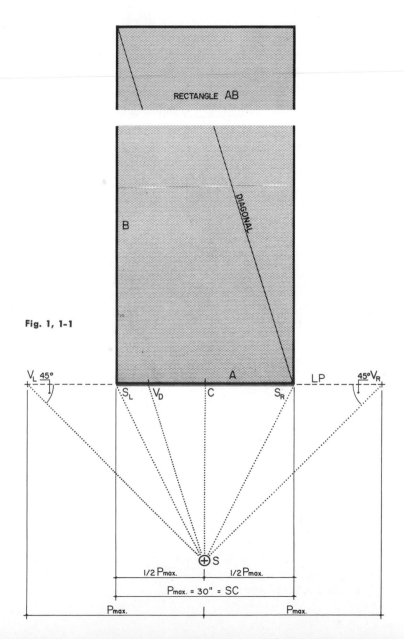

Fig. 1, 1-1

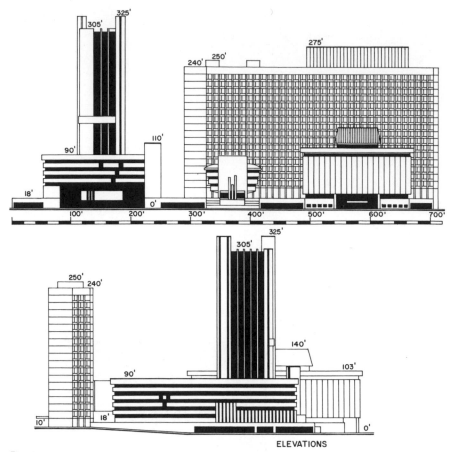

ELEVATIONS

Fig. 1, 1-2

Preparation of the Site Plan

Enclose that part of the object to be illustrated by drawing the rectangle AB. Measure its sides A and B in any scale in order to obtain the ratio $A:B$, provided that A and B are measured in the same scale. In this demonstration the ratio is $A:B = 140':450' \approx 5:16$.

P_{max}, the maximal size of the perspective, is 30 in. wide, and $H_p = {}^3\!/_4 P_{max} = 22.5$ in. high. It is recommended that this perspective be constructed on a board twice as long as P_{max}, or 60 in. This eases the layout of a grid system by employing 45° diagonals and their vanishing points.

1.* Draw the outline of the perspective 30 in. wide $= P_{max} = 140$ ft, and 22.5 in. high $= H_p = 105$ ft. Mark the left vertical S_L and the right vertical S_R.

2. Draw a horizon not higher than $\frac{1}{4} P_{max}$; i.e., $H_H = \frac{1}{4} \times 30$ in. $= 7.5$ in. $= 35$ ft, measured from the groundline A to intersect S_L and S_R. Bisect the distance between S_L and S_R to locate the center and vanishing point V_C of the perspective at the horizon.

3. Draw perspective lines to V_C from the intersections of A with S_L and S_R.

4. Locate the rear side A of the rectangle AB by employing the formula

$$V_D V_C = \frac{A}{B} SC$$

$$SC = (H_p - H_H)\,2 = (105' - 35')\,2$$
$$= 140' = 30'' = P_{max}$$

*Throughout this book, numbered steps in text correspond to circled numbers in the illustrations.

8

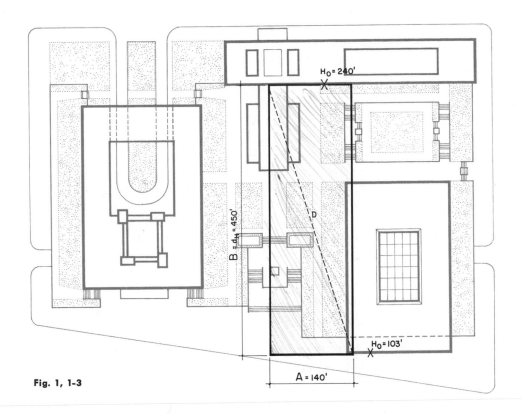

Fig. 1, 1-3

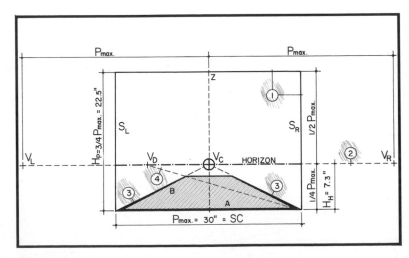

Fig. 1, 1-4

V_D is the vanishing point of the diagonal of AB and has to be scaled off from V_C to the left or the right side. In the case of the illustrated perspective,

$$V_D V_C = \frac{140'}{450'}\, 30'' = 9.33''$$

The determinant factor of this equation is the ratio $A:B$. If it is employed superficially, the perspective will be distorted; for instance, if the reciprocal value $B:A$ is used, then the proportion of the rectangle will be perspectively reversed. Draw the perspective line from one of the front corners of AB to V_D to intersect one of the perspective lines converging in $V_D V_C$. The intersection determines the location of the rear side A. Draw the horizontal to complete the perspective layout of AB.

Note: If very high objects have to be projected, it might be advisable to apply the bird's-eye perspective (see Fig. 2, 1-4). In this case the maximum width $P_{\max}$ equals only two-thirds of the distance between the station point S and the center C of the perspective; i.e., $P_{\max} = \tfrac{2}{3}SC$.

The Completion of the Perspective

As mentioned before under the $P_{\max}$ projection, the perspective is 30 in. wide and 22.5 in. high. In this demonstration $P_{\max} = 30$ in. is the equivalent of side $A = 140$ ft, and consequently $H_p = 22.5$ in. is the equivalent of 105 ft. The height of the horizon was established with $\tfrac{1}{4} \times 30$ in. $= 7.5$ in., the equivalent of 35 ft.

1. Calibrate either the left or the right side of the perspective to 105 or 10.5 units, whichever is more convenient (see Fig. 1, 1-5, Fig. 1, 1-7, and Fig. 1, 1-8).

2. Lay off diverse sections of side B from the left to the right in any suitable scale, continue according to Chap. 3, Method 2, and draw horizontals on the groundline where necessary.

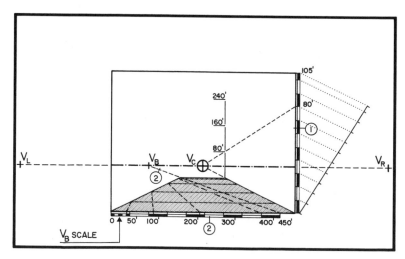

Fig. 1, 1-5

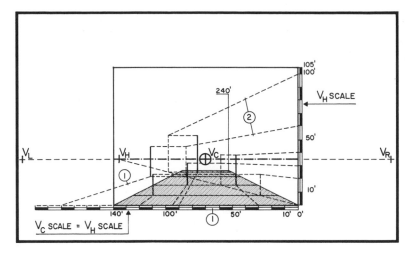

Fig. 1, 1-6

1. The groundline of the perspective is 30 in. long and represents the side $A = 140$ ft of the rectangle AB. Calibrate the groundline by the vertical side of the perspective. If the calibration of this side is correct, the groundline should measure up to whatever length A may be, in this particular example 140 ft. This process offers a chance to countercheck the accuracy of the vertical scale. Draw perspective lines from the diverse sections at the groundline to V_C in order to intersect the horizontals and to position the floor plan of the object (see perspective Fig. 1, 1-7).

2. Transfer the diverse heights from the vertical scale to the appropriate points in accordance with the instructions in Chap. 3, Method 5, and complete the perspective layout (see perspective Fig. 1, 1-8).

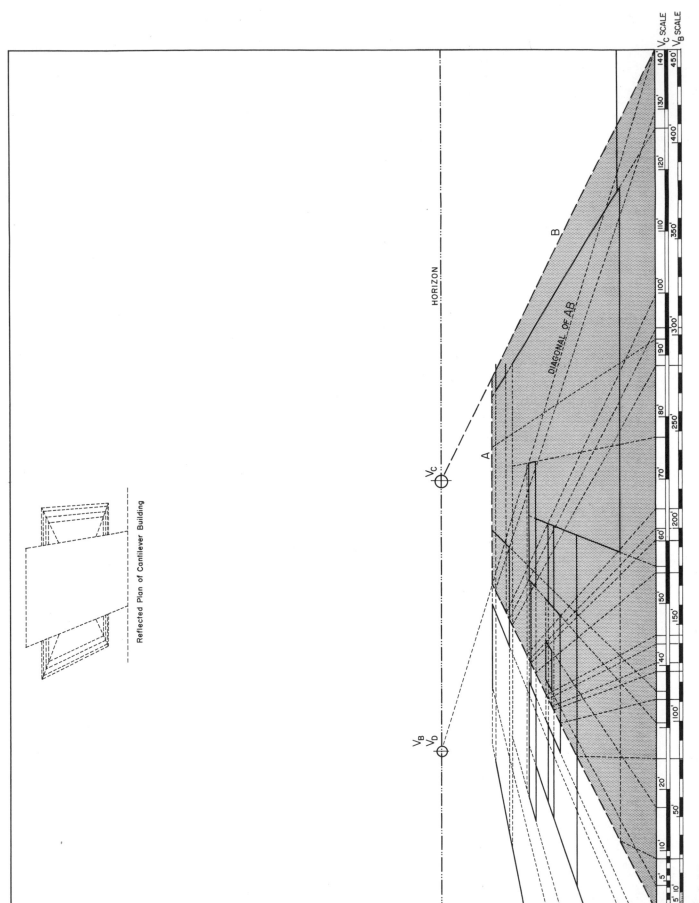

Reflected Plan of Cantilever Building

HORIZON

V_C

V_B
V_D

A

B

DIAGONAL OF AB

V_C SCALE

V_B SCALE

Fig. 1, 1-7

to VR →

VH SCALE

100'
90'
80'
70'
60'
50'
40'
30'
20'
10'

V_C

V_H

METHOD 2: Picture Plane
Parallel to the Diagonal of AB

Characteristics

The diagonal D of the rectangle AB is parallel to the picture plane (see Fig. 1, 2-1); hence, D determines the position of AB to the picture plane LP. This limits the use of the method which is bound to the ratio $A:B \leq 2:1$, and $A:B \geq 1:2$; i.e., the side A cannot be longer than $2B$ and not shorter than $\frac{1}{2}B$. If this ratio is disregarded, only one side of the object appears in the perspective.

The maximal width P_{max} equals the distance from the station point S to the center C and is determined by the equation

$$P_{max} = SC = \frac{T}{A/B + B/A}$$

The central line of vision SC intersects the total span $V_L V_R = T$ in C. The distance between the left vanishing point V_L and C is set by the equation

$$V_L C = \frac{A}{B} SC$$

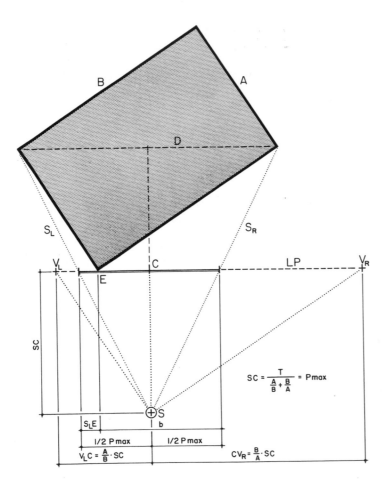

$$SC = \frac{T}{\frac{A}{B} + \frac{B}{A}} = Pmax$$

Fig. 1, 2-1

14

Consequently

$$CV_R = \frac{B}{A} SC$$

locating C, the center of the perspective.

The height of the object at its point of intersection with the picture plane LP has to be equal to or less than $\frac{3}{4}P_{max}$.

$$H_o = H_p \leq \frac{3}{4}P_{max}$$

The point of contact of AB is E, located by the construction itself (see DETERMINATION OF THE LOCATION OF POINT E, step 2, page 20).

Applicability

Any object can be projected as long as side A remains smaller than $2B$ and longer than $\frac{1}{2}B$. The designer is responsible for shaping AB in this fashion without changing the proportions of the object, because the rectangle AB is a frame into which any object can be fitted. The restriction does not apply to a bird's-eye perspective.

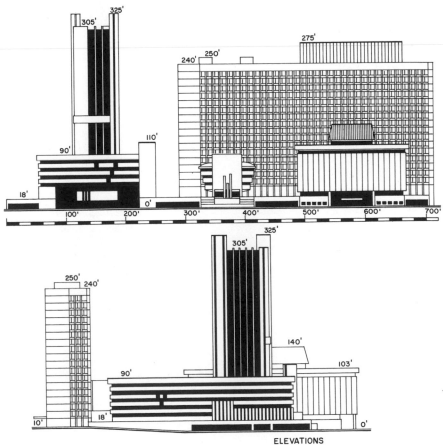

ELEVATIONS

Fig. 1, 2-2

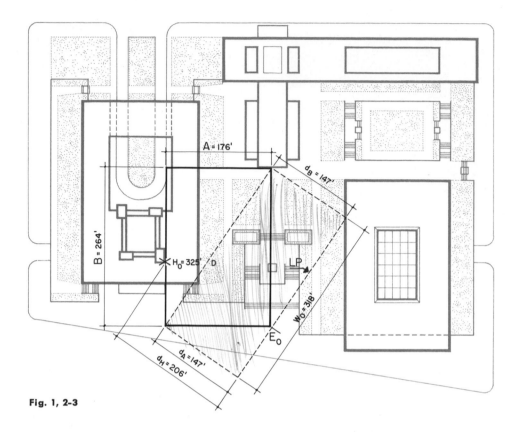

Fig. 1, 2-3

Preparation of the Site Plan

(According to Chap. 3, Method 6.)

1. Enclose that part of the object to be illustrated by the rectangle AB (see Fig. 1, 2-3), making side A shorter than $2B$ and longer than $\frac{1}{2}B$, and draw the diagonal D. Then measure the sides A and B in any scale in order to obtain the ratio $A:B$. In this demonstration $A:B = 176':264' = 2:3$.

2. To determine whether the P_{max} projection or the P_H projection should be used, draw the line LP in the site plan through the foremost corner E_o of AB (in this demonstration parallel to the diagonal D) and drop the perpendiculars d_A and d_B upon LP (see Fig. 1, 2-3a). The distance between d_A and d_B is W_o. To the scale of the site plan scale off $d_A = 147$ ft, $d_B = 147$ ft, and $W_o = 318$ ft; then deduct one-half of d_A and d_B from W_o in order to obtain $P_{o,max}$; i.e.,

$$P_{o,max} = W_o - \frac{1}{2}(d_A + d_B)$$

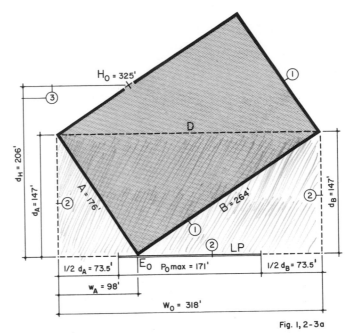

Fig. I, 2-3a

Fig. 1, 2-3a

3. Mark the highest point of the object X and scale off $d_H = 206$ ft, the plumb distance between X and LP. Deduct from $H_o = 325$ ft the height of the object at X, $\frac{1}{2}d_H = \frac{1}{2} \times 206$ ft, plus the height of the horizon $H_H = 74$ ft, which should be determined by this time and should not exceed $\frac{1}{3}H_o$ (see Fig. 1, 2-2).

$$H_o - (\tfrac{1}{2}d_H + H_H) = 325' - (103' + 74') = 148' = \tfrac{1}{2}SC_o$$

SC_o is the distance between the center of the perspective C_o and the station point S_o in the site plan.

CONCLUSION: $SC_o = 296$ ft exceeds $P_{o,max} = 171$ ft by more than 10 percent; therefore $P_{o,max}$ has to be reduced to P_H by applying the P_H projection (see P_H: THE MAXIMAL WIDTH OF THE PERSPECTIVE FOR HIGH OBJECTS.)

If SC_o is less than $P_{o,max}$, then the P_{max} projection must be used.

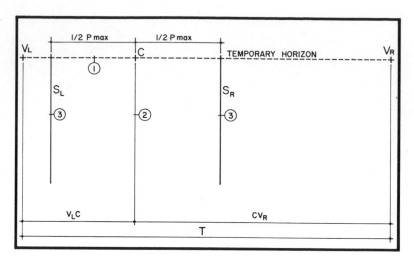

Fig. 1, 2-4

P_{max}: **the Maximal Size of the Perspective**

1. Draw a temporary horizon on the upper part of the drawing board, mark the ends V_L and V_R, and drop perpendiculars from them.

2. Scale off T and derive P_{max} and SC by applying the formula

$$P_{\text{max}} = SC = \frac{T}{A/B + B/A}$$

Locate the center of the perspective by the formulas

$$V_L C = \frac{A}{B}\, SC$$

$$CV_R = \frac{B}{A}\, SC$$

3. Lay off $\frac{1}{2}P_{\text{max}}$ to the left and to the right of C, drop perpendiculars from these points, and mark them S_L and S_R. They represent the left and right sidelines of the perspective.

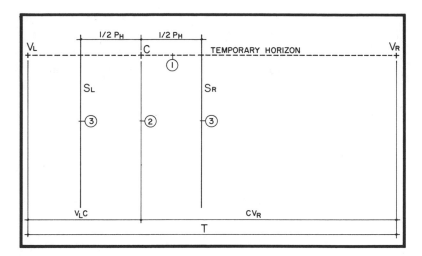

Fig. 1, 2-5

P_H: the Maximal Width of the Perspective for High Objects

(See Chap. 3, Method 6.)

1.) Draw a horizontal line as a temporary horizon at a convenient height across the drawing board and locate the vanishing points V_L and V_R. Scale off in inches the distance T between V_L and V_R. For this demonstration the distance has been set at 60 in. Derive SC, the distance between the station point S and the center of the perspective C, by employing the formula

$$SC = \frac{T}{A/B + B/A} = \frac{60''}{2/3 + 3/2} = 27.7''$$

2.) Using either of the following formulas,

$$V_L C = \frac{A}{B} SC$$

$$CV_R = \frac{B}{A} SC$$

locate the center of the perspective.

$$V_L C = \tfrac{2}{3} \times 27.7'' = 18.5''$$

or

$$CV_R = \tfrac{3}{2} \times 27.7'' = 41.5''$$

3.) Derive the maximum width P_H by the formula

$$\tfrac{1}{2}P_H = \frac{W_o}{d_A + 2SC_o + d_B} SC$$

$$= \frac{318'}{147' + 592' + 147'} 27.7'' = 0.36'' \times 27.7'' \approx 10''$$

Lay off $\tfrac{1}{2}P_H$ to the left and to the right of C, locating S_L and S_R, and erect verticals, which are the sidelines of the perspective. From here follow DETERMINATION OF THE LOCATION OF POINT E.

Determination of the Location of Point E

To construct the perspective in accordance with the proportions of the rectangle AB and its position to the picture plane, it is essential to determine properly E, the point at which the nearest corner of the rectangle touches the picture plane.

1. Draw the horizontal from S_L to S_R at a convenient height.
2. Draw perspective lines from V_L and V_R through the intersections of the horizontal with S_L and S_R in order to locate E at the intersection of the perspective lines.
3. Erect the vertical at E.

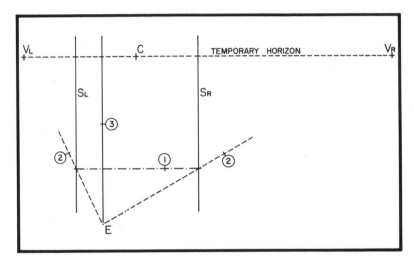

Fig. 1, 2-6

Final Adjustment of the Horizon

Since the size of the perspective was based upon the length of the available drawing board or was chosen by the designer, its scale has to be derived from the construction of the perspective in order to establish the respective height of the object. Use one of the three solutions in Chap. 3, Method 4.

Applying Method 4, Solution c:

1. Bisect the section S_LS_R of the temporary horizon and mark it C; then draw a line from E_G to C.
2. Drop a perpendicular from C in order to bisect the horizontal S_LS_R at M and draw a semicircle over this horizontal.
3. Erect the vertical at the intersection of the horizontal and the line E_GC in order to intersect the semicircle.
4. Rotate the point of this intersection from the intersection of E_GV_L and S_L upward to locate side A upon S_L.

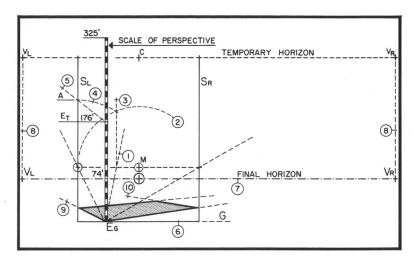

Fig. 1, 2-7

5. Project side A upon the vertical at E by drawing the perspective line from V_L through A upon S_L until it intersects the vertical at E and mark it E_T. The section $E_G E_T$ on the vertical E is the true length of side $A = 176$ ft upon the picture plane. Divide $E_G E_T$ into 176 units, or any convenient scale, and continue upward until reaching 325 units. This is the height of the highest point of the object, which is marked X in Fig. 1, 2-3.

6. Draw the horizontal G from S_L to S_R through E_G.

7. Draw final horizon 74 ft above G, as determined by step 2, PREPARATION OF THE SITE PLAN, page 16.

8. Transfer temporary V_L and V_R to the final horizon by dropping perpendiculars.

9. Draw perspective lines from E_G to V_L and V_R on the final horizon.

10. Complete the perspective of AB by drawing perspective lines from S_L to V_R and from S_R to V_L.

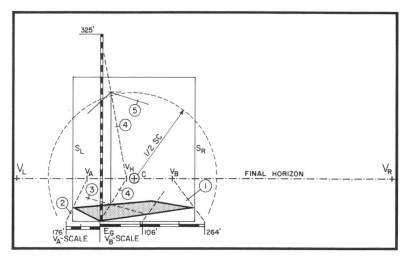

Fig. 1, 2-8

Completion of the Perspective

1. Beginning at E_G, lay off the various sections of side B to the right in any suitable scale and continue according to Chap. 3, Method 2, in order to project these sections upon $E_G V_R$.

2. Repeat every step to the left of E in order to locate the perspectively reduced sections of side A on $V_L E_G$ (see Fig. 1, 2-8 and the perspective Fig. 1, 2-9).

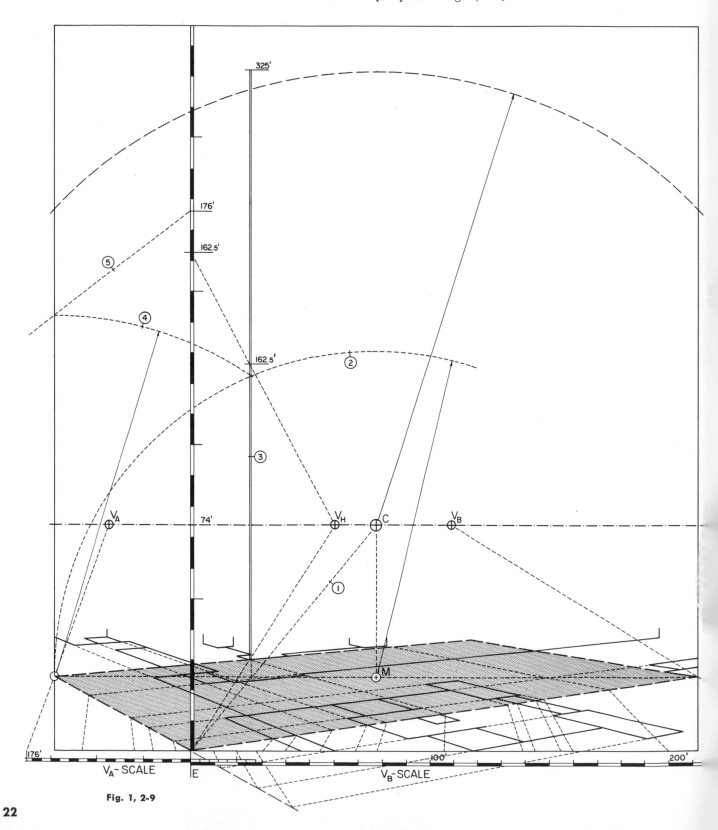

Fig. 1, 2-9

3. Draw perspective lines from the sections of $V_L E_G$ to V_R and from $E_G V_R$ to V_L to locate the corners of the object.

4. Erect verticals at the points of all corners of the object and transfer the respective heights from the scale at E (see Chap. 3, Method 5).

5. Complete the perspective by drawing perspective lines from various heights of the object (see Fig. 1, 2-10).

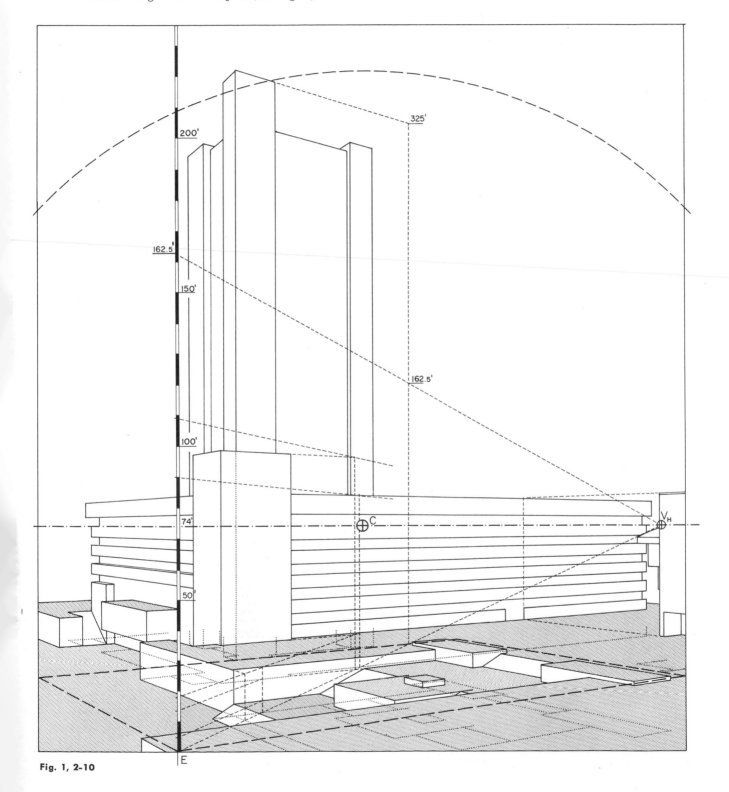

Fig. 1, 2-10

23

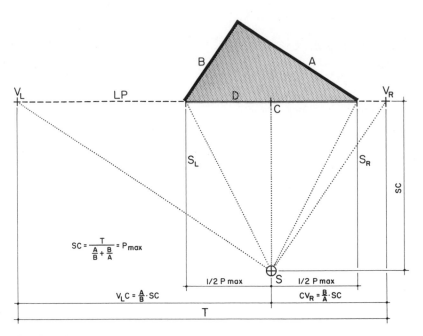

Fig. 1, 3a-1

In the figure:

$$SC = \frac{T}{\frac{A}{B} + \frac{B}{A}} = P_{max}$$

$$V_LC = \frac{A}{B} \cdot SC$$

$$CV_R = \frac{B}{A} \cdot SC$$

METHOD 3a: The Hypotenuse of the Triangle *ABD* is the Picture Plane

Characteristics

The part of the object to be illustrated is enclosed by the right triangle ABD. Its hypotenuse D is the picture plane; i.e., D equals P_{max}, the maximum width of the perspective, which is also the distance SC between the station point S and the center C of the perspective.

$$D = P_{max} = SC$$

The central line of vision SC intersects the total span $T = V_L V_R$ in C (see Fig. 1, 3a-1).

The maximal width of the perspective $P_{max} = SC$ is determined by the equation

$$P_{max} = SC = \frac{T}{A/B + B/A}$$

The distance between the left vanishing point V_L and C and the distance between C and the right vanishing point V_R are

$$V_L C = \frac{A}{B} SC$$

$$CV_R = \frac{B}{A} SC$$

The height of the object H_o at its intersection with the picture plane LP has to be equal to or less than $\frac{3}{4}D = \frac{3}{4}P_{max}$.

The point E is behind the picture plane and has to be located by the construction of the perspective (see DETERMINATION OF THE LOCATION OF POINT E, page 29).

Any object of which one inner corner has to be pictured can be projected by this method as long as $A:B$ is less than 2 but more than $1:2$.

Note: If the ratio $A:B$ is more than 2 or less than $1:2$, then follow the instructions given in Method $3b$ (page 34).

Recommended for plazas, squares, courtyards, and interiors.

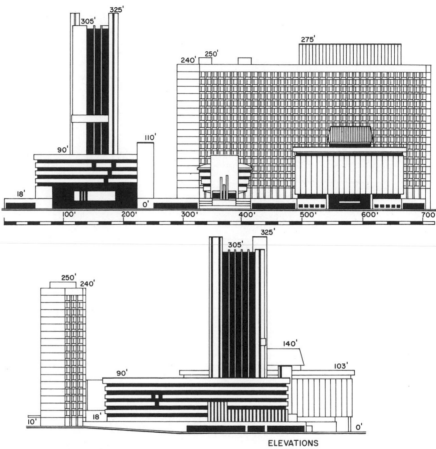

ELEVATIONS

Fig. 1, 3a-2

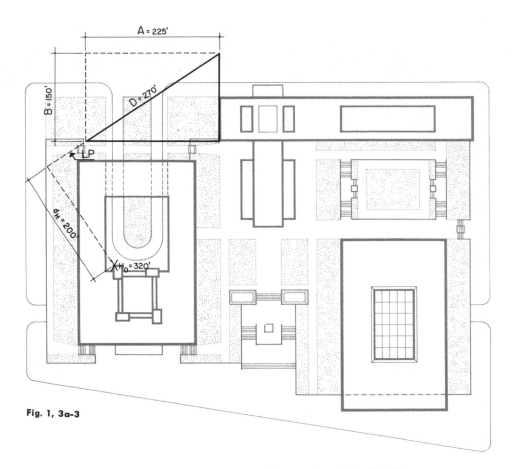

Fig. 1, 3a-3

Preparation of the Site Plan

1. Enclose that part of the object to be illustrated by drawing the right triangle ABD (see Fig. 1, 3a-3). Measure its sides A and B in the same scale in order to obtain the ratio $A:B$. In this demonstration the ratio is $225':150' = 3:2$. The diagonal D measures 270 ft according to the site plan, whereas the height H_o equals 320 ft (see Fig. 1, 3a-2), which is more than $\frac{3}{4}D = \frac{3}{4} \times 270$ ft $= 200$ ft. See and compare H_o in CHARACTERISTICS. Consequently more information from the site plan is needed in order to decide which projection should be applied, the $P_{\max}$ projection or the P_H projection for high objects (see Chap. 3, Method 6).

2. Scale off the right angular distance $d_H = 200$ ft between X and D to the scale of the site plan and deduct one-half of it from $H_o = 320$ ft; i.e.,

$$H_p = H_o - \tfrac{1}{2}d_H = 320' - \tfrac{1}{2} \times 200' = 220'$$

H_p is the projected height upon the picture plane.

Determine the height of the horizon H_H, keeping in mind that it should not exceed one-third of H_p:

$$\tfrac{1}{3}H_p = \tfrac{1}{3} \times 220' = 73.3'$$

In this demonstration $H_H = 52$ ft. Deduct H_H from H_p to obtain $\frac{1}{2}SC_o$.

$$\tfrac{1}{2}SC_o = H_p - H_H = 220' - 52' = 168'$$

hence

$$SC_o = 336'$$

SC_o is the distance between C_o, the center of D, and the station point S on the site plan.

CONCLUSION: $SC_o = 336$ ft exceeds $D = 270$ ft $= P_{o,\max}$ by more than 10 percent; therefore $P_{o,\max}$ has to be reduced to P_H by applying the P_H projection. Follow the instructions for P_H: THE MAXIMAL WIDTH OF THE PERSPECTIVE FOR HIGH OBJECTS.

If SC_o is less than $P_{o,\max}$, then the $P_{\max}$ projection should be used.

$P_{\max}$: the Maximal Size of the Perspective

1. Draw a temporary horizon on the upper part of the drawing board and locate the vanishing points V_L and V_R.
2. Scale off in inches the distance T between V_L and V_R. Derive $P_{\max} = SC$ by the formula

$$P_{\max} = SC = \frac{T}{A/B + B/A}$$

Locate the center C of the perspective by the formulas

$$V_L C = \frac{A}{B} SC$$

$$C V_R = \frac{B}{A} SC$$

3. Lay off one-half $P_{\max}$ to the left and to the right of C in order to locate the sidelines S_L and S_R of the perspective and drop perpendiculars. Then follow the instructions for DETERMINATION OF THE LOCATION OF POINT E.

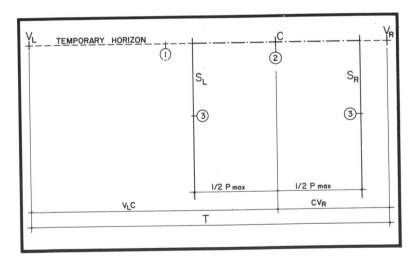

Fig. 1, 3a-4

P_H: the Maximal Width of the Perspective for High Objects

1. Draw a temporary horizon on the upper part of the drawing board, locate the vanishing points V_L and V_R, and scale off in inches the distance T between V_L and V_R. For this demonstration the distance is set at 60 in. Derive SC by the formula

$$SC = \frac{T}{A/B + B/A} = \frac{60''}{3/2 + 2/3} = \frac{60''}{2.17} = 27.6''$$

2. Locate C, the center of the perspective, by the formula

$$V_L C = \frac{A}{B} SC = \tfrac{3}{2} \times 27.6'' = 41.5''$$

$$CV_R = \frac{B}{A} SC = \tfrac{2}{3} \times 27.6'' = 18.5''$$

$$T = 60''$$

3. Derive P_H by the formula $P_H = SC/f$.

$$f = \frac{SC_o}{D} = \frac{336'}{270'} \approx 1.25$$

(See PREPARATION OF THE SITE PLAN.)
Lay off $\tfrac{1}{2} P_H = 11$ in. to the left and to the right of C in order to locate the sidelines S_L and S_R and drop perpendiculars. From here on follow the instructions for DETERMINATION OF THE LOCATION OF POINT E.

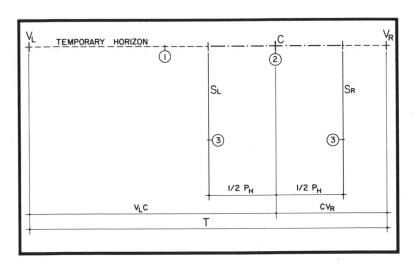

Fig. 1, 3a-5

28

Determination of the Location of Point *E*

1. Draw the horizontal G, which is the side D of ABD, from S_L to S_R on the lower part of the drawing board.
2. Draw perspective lines from S_L to V_R and from S_R to V_L, locating E at their intersection.

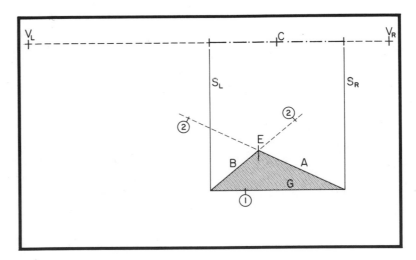

Fig. 1, 3a-6

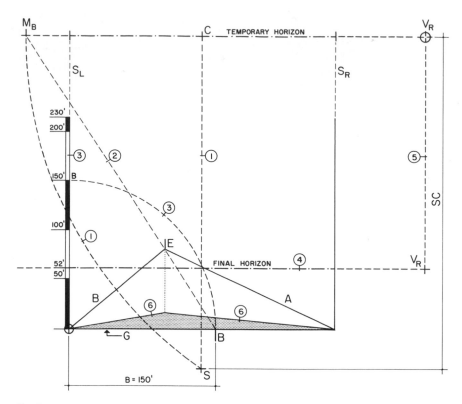

Fig. 1, 3a-7

Final Adjustment of the Horizon

The adequate scale of this perspective has to be derived from the construction of the perspective itself, because its size was based upon the length of the drawing board or was chosen by the designer. Use one of the three solutions presented in Chap. 3, Method 4.

Applying Method 4, Solution *a* in this demonstration:

1. Drop a perpendicular from C; lay off $SC = 27.6$ in. from C downward, locating S; then rotate SV_R from V_R upward to locate M_B at the temporary horizon.

2. Connect M_B with E, passing through E in order to locate B on the groundline G. The distance between S_L and B is the adequate length of side B and represents 150 ft (see site plan Fig. 1, 3a-3).

3. Rotate B from S_L at G upward to locate the 150-ft mark on the vertical S_L. Divide this vertical with respective units up to the 150-ft mark and continue upward until reaching the 230-ft mark, which is the height of the building on the left side.

4. Draw final horizon at the 52-ft mark, which is the previously determined height H_H of the horizon (see PREPARATION OF THE SITE PLAN, page 26).

5. Transfer V_L and V_R to the final horizon by dropping perpendiculars from the temporary horizon.

6. Lay out the final shape of ABD by drawing perspective lines from S_R to V_L and from S_L to V_R on the final horizon.

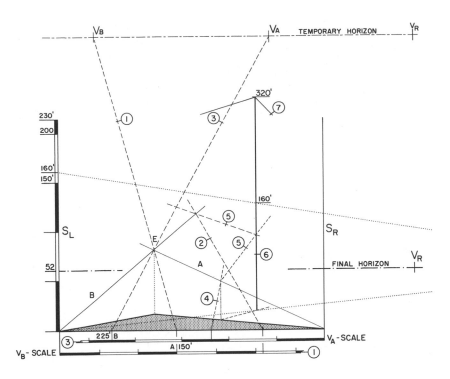

Fig. 1, 3a-8

Completion of the Perspective

1. Lay off various sections of side B, including those beyond the A mark, from S_L to the right in any suitable scale (see Fig. 1, 3a-3). Draw a connecting line from the A mark to E and continue in order to locate V_B at the horizon.

2. Draw lines from each section of the V_B scale to V_B to project these sections perspectively upon B (see perspective Fig. 1, 3a-9).

3. Lay off various sections of the side A, including those beyond the B mark (see Fig. 1, 3a-3), from S_R to the left; then draw a connecting line from the B mark to E and continue in order to locate V_A at the horizon.

4. Draw lines from each section of the V_A scale to V_A to project these sections perspectively upon A (see perspective Fig. 1, 3a-9).

   Note: V_A and V_B are not true vanishing points. They are temporary, necessary only for the projection of the A and B sections.

5. Draw perspective lines from the A sections to V_R and from the B sections to V_L to locate specific corners of the object (see perspective Fig. 1, 3a-9).

   Note: In this demonstration the horizon is 52 ft high. If the height of the horizon were only 5.2 ft, it would be impossible to "zero-in" an intersection of two perspective lines coming from V_L and V_R between G and the horizon. To overcome this problem, the triangle ABD can be drawn upside down with the measure lines at the top of the perspective, as demonstrated in the upper part of Fig. 1, 3a-9. Here, the intersections of the perspective lines are clear and easy to read. Therefore it can be stated that the greater the distance between measure line and horizon, the clearer the intersection of two perspective lines. Another way to obtain exact intersections is the use of the preliminary horizon and the auxiliary triangle ABD, as shown in Figs. 1, 3a-7 and 3a-8.

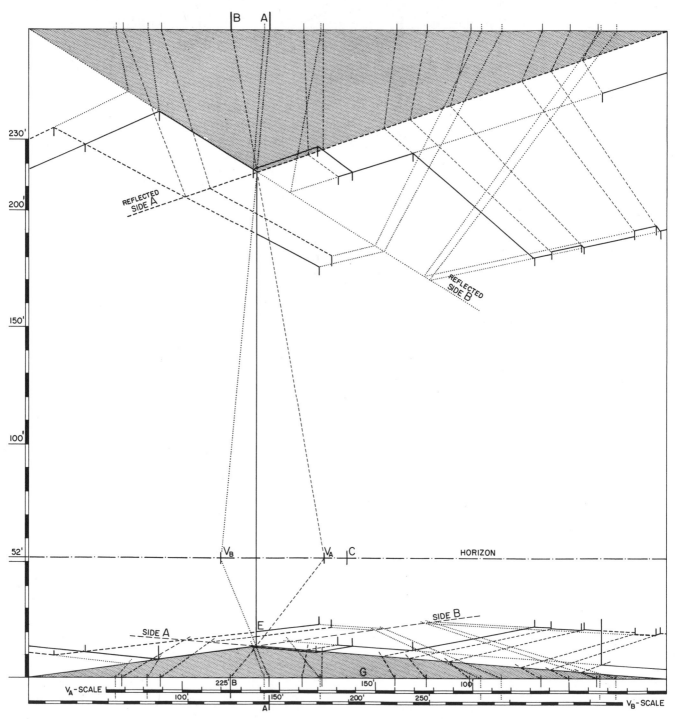

Fig. 1, 3a-9

6. Erect verticals at sections of *A* and *B* and at the intersections of the perspective lines; then transfer the respective heights from the scale at S_L to the appropriate verticals, applying Method 5 in Chap. 3.
7. Complete the perspective by drawing perspective lines from various heights of the object to V_L and V_R (see perspective Fig. 1, 3a-10).

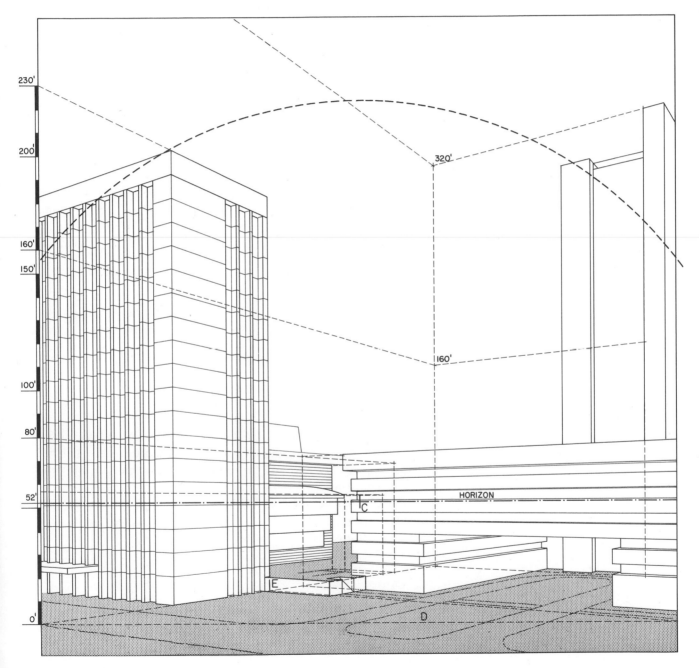

Fig. 1, 3a-10

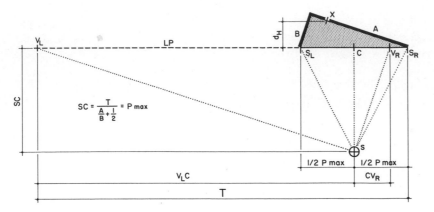

Fig. 1, 3b-1

METHOD 3b: The Hypotenuse of the Triangle ABD is the Picture Plane with One Vanishing Point within the Perspective

Characteristics

The part of the object to be illustrated is enclosed by the right triangle ABD. Its hypotenuse D is the picture plane; i.e., D equals P_{max}, the maximal width of the perspective, which is also the distance SC between the station point S and the center C of the perspective.

$$D = P_{max} = SC$$

The central line of vision SC intersects the total span T in C (see Fig. 1, 3b-1), therefore

$$T = V_L V_R + V_R S_R \qquad \text{or} \qquad T = S_L V_L + V_L V_R$$

The maximal width of the perspective $P_{max} = SC$ is determined by the equation

$$P_{max} = SC = \frac{T}{A/B + 1/2}$$

Note: In the ratio $A{:}B$ of this formula A *and* B *can switch* from numerator to denominator. In this demonstration side A is the larger side, hence, $A{:}B$. If, however, B is larger than $2A$, the ratio consequently becomes $B{:}A$.

The distance between the left vanishing point V_L and C is set by the equations

$$V_L C = \frac{A}{B} SC$$

$$CV_R = \frac{B}{A} SC$$

Attention: In these two formulas *the position of A and B in the ratios A:B and B:A is fixed.*

The height H_o of the object at its intersection with the picture plane *LP* has to be equal to or less than $\frac{3}{4}D = \frac{3}{4}P_{max}$.

The point *E* is behind the picture plane and has to be located by the construction of the perspective (see DETERMINATION OF THE LOCATION OF POINT E, page 39).

Applicability

Any object of which *one* or even *two inner* corners have to be pictured can be projected by this method, as long as $A:B$ is more than 2 or less than $\frac{1}{2}$. Recommended for plazas, squares, courtyards, and interiors.

See Method 1, 3a, demonstrating the condition of $A:B$ less than 2 but more than $\frac{1}{2}$.

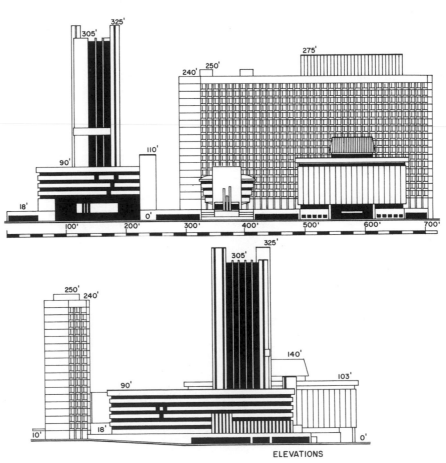

ELEVATIONS

Fig. 1, 3b-2

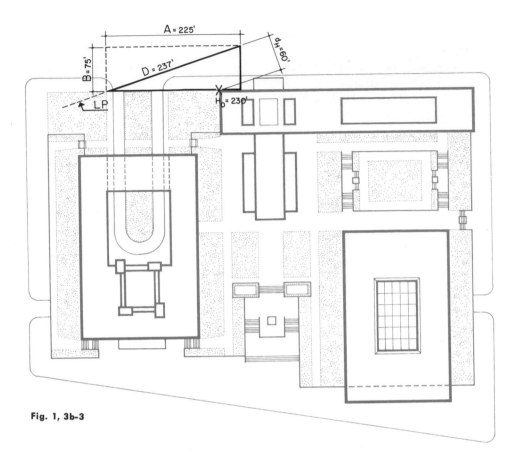

Fig. 1, 3b-3

Preparation of the Site Plan

1. Enclose that part of the object to be illustrated by drawing the right triangle DAB (see Fig. 1, $3b$-3). Measure its sides A and B in any scale, provided that the same scale is used for both, in order to obtain the ratio $A:B$. In this demonstration the ratio is $225':75' = 3:1$.

   The diagonal D measures 237 ft, according to the scale of the site plan, whereas the height of the highest part X of the object is $H_o = 230$ ft (see Fig. 1, $3b$-2). This is greater than $\frac{3}{4}D = \frac{3}{4} \times 237$ ft $= 178$ ft. Compare H_o in CHARACTERISTICS. Therefore, more accurate information from the site plan is needed in order to decide whether the $P_{\max}$ projection or the P_H projection for high objects should be applied.

2. Scale off the right angular distance d_H between X and D to the scale of the site plan and deduct one-half of it from $H_o = 230$ ft; i.e.,

$$H_p = H_o - \tfrac{1}{2}d_H = 230' - \tfrac{1}{2} \times 60' = 200'$$

H_p is the projected height upon the picture plane. Determine the height of the horizon H_H, keeping in mind that it should not exceed $\frac{1}{3}H_p = \frac{1}{3} \times 200$ ft $= 66.6$ ft. In this demonstration it is 52 ft. Deduct H_H from H_p to obtain $\frac{1}{2}SC_o$.

$$\tfrac{1}{2}SC_o = H_p - H_H = 200' - 52' = 148'$$

hence

$$SC_o = 296'$$

SC_o is the distance between C_o, the center of D, and the station point S on the site plan. $D = P_{o,\max} = 237$ ft. See note following COMPLETION OF THE PERSPECTIVE, page 41.

CONCLUSION: SC_o exceeds $D = P_{o,\max}$ by more than 10 percent; therefore $P_{o,\max}$ has to be reduced to P_H by applying the P_H projection (see P_H: THE MAXIMAL WIDTH OF THE PERSPECTIVE FOR HIGH OBJECTS).

If SC_o is less than $P_{o,\max}$, then the $P_{\max}$ projection must be used.

$P_{\max}$: the Maximal Size of the Perspective

1. Draw a temporary horizon on the upper part of the drawing board and locate the vanishing point V_L and the right sideline S_R of the perspective, or $S_L V_R$, when $A:B$ is less than $1:2$.

2. Scale off in inches the distance T between V_L and S_R and derive $P_{\max} = SC$ by the formula

$$P_{\max} = SC = \frac{T}{A/B + 1/2}$$

Lay off $P_{\max}$ to the left of S_R in order to locate S_L and drop perpendiculars from S_L and S_R. Bisect $S_L S_R$, locating C, the center of the perspective.

3. To locate the right vanishing point V_R, derive CV_R by the formula

$$CV_R = \frac{B}{A} SC$$

From here follow the instructions for DETERMINATION OF THE LOCATION OF POINT E.

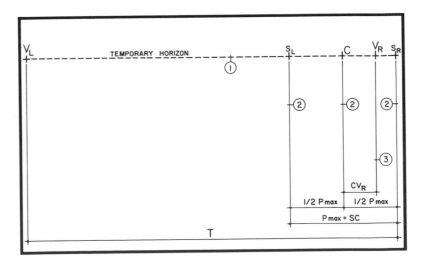

Fig. 1, 3b-4

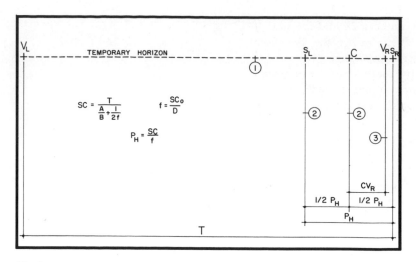

Fig. 1, 3b-5

P_H: **the Maximal Width of the Perspective for High Objects**

1. Draw a temporary horizon on the upper part of the drawing board; locate the vanishing point V_L and the right sideline S_R of the perspective. Scale off in inches the distance T between V_L and S_R. For this demonstration $T = 60$ in.

   Derive SC by the formula

   $$SC = \frac{T}{A/B + 1/2 \times 1/f}$$

   Note: The application of this formula is limited to the maximum of f; i.e.,

   $$f_{max} = \frac{1}{2}\frac{A}{B}$$

   If $f = \dfrac{SC_o}{D}$ exceeds $\frac{1}{2}A/B$ the original formula

   $$SC = T/(A/B + B/A)$$

   has to be applied to determine SC.

   $$f = \frac{SC_o}{D} = \frac{296'}{237'} \approx 1.25$$

   $$SC = \frac{60''}{3/1 + 1/2 \times 1/1.25} = \frac{60''}{3.4} = 17.6''$$

2. Derive P_H by the formula

   $$P_H = \frac{SC}{f} = \frac{17.6''}{1.25} = 14.2''$$

   Lay off $P_H = 14.2$ in. to the left side of S_R, marking it S_L; bisect $S_L S_R$, locating C; and drop perpendiculars from S_L, C, and S_R.

3. Derive CV_R in order to locate the right vanishing point V_R.

   $$CV_R = \frac{B}{A} SC = \frac{1}{3} \times 17.6'' = 5.9''$$

   Lay off CV_R to the right of C and mark it V_R. From here follow the instructions for DETERMINATION OF THE LOCATION OF POINT E.

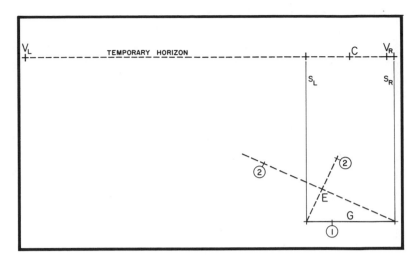

Fig. 1, 3b-6

Determination of the Location of Point E

1. Draw the groundline G from S_L to S_R on the lower part of the drawing board.
2. Draw perspective lines from S_L to V_R and from S_R to V_L, locating E at their intersection.

Final Adjustment of the Horizon

The adequate scale of this perspective has to be derived by the construction of the perspective, because its size was based upon the length of the drawing board or was chosen by the designer. Use one of the three solutions in Chap. 3, Method 4.

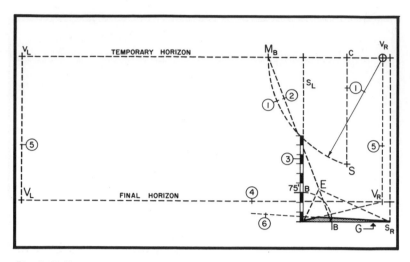

Fig. 1, 3b-7

Applying here Method 4, Solution *a*:

1. Drop the perpendicular from *C*; lay off $SC = 17.6$ in. from *C* downward, locating *S*; then rotate SV_R from V_R upward to locate M_B at the temporary horizon.

2. Connect M_B with *E*, passing through *E* in order to locate *B* on the groundline *G*. The distance between S_L and *B* is the adequate length of the side *B* and represents 75 ft (see site plan Fig. 1, 3*b*-3).

3. Rotate *B* from S_L at *G* upward to locate the 75-ft mark on the vertical S_L. Divide this vertical into respective units up to the 75-ft mark and continue upward until reaching the 230-ft mark.

4. Draw final horizon at the 52-ft mark, which is the previously determined height H_H of the horizon (see PREPARATION OF THE SITE PLAN, page 36).

5. Transfer V_L and V_R to the final horizon by dropping perpendiculars from the temporary horizon.

6. Lay out the final shape of *ABD* by drawing perspective lines from S_R to V_L and from S_L to V_R on the final horizon.

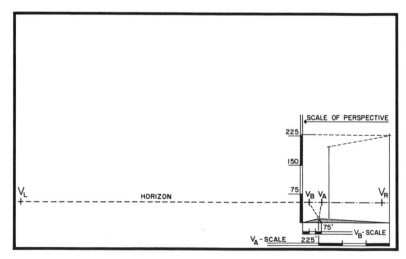

Fig. 1, 3b-8

Completion of the Perspective

1. Lay off various sections of side B, including those beyond the A mark (see Fig. 1, $3b$-9), from S_L to the right in any suitable scale. Draw connecting lines from the A mark to E and continue in order to locate V_B at the horizon.

2. Draw lines from each section to V_B to project them perspectively upon side A (see Fig. 1, $3b$-9).

3. Lay off various sections of the side A, including those beyond the B mark (see Fig. 1, $3b$-9), from S_R to the left; then draw a connecting line from the B mark to E and continue in order to locate V_A at the horizon.

4. Draw lines from each section to V_A to project them perspectively upon side B (see Fig. 1, $3b$-9).

   Note: V_A and V_B are not true vanishing points. They are temporary, necessary only for the projection of the A and B sections.

5. Draw perspective lines from the sections of side A to V_R and from the sections of side B to V_L to locate specific corners of the object (see Fig. 1, $3b$-9).

6. Erect verticals at the intersections of the perspective lines; then transfer the respective heights from the scale at S_L to the appropriate verticals, applying Method 5 in Chap. 3.

7. Complete the perspective by drawing perspective lines from the various heights of the object to V_L and V_R (see Fig. 1, $3b$-10).

Note: See Fig. 1, $3b$-10. The high tower in the rear appears distorted and is, in fact, distorted, because it exceeds the circle of undistorted projection and lies above the vanishing point V_R. This situation can be avoided by moving the sector of view to the right, thus bringing the tower more into the center, or by moving it to the left, cutting off the right corner of the tower by the sideline of the perspective; i.e., hiding the distortion or reducing width and height of the perspective proportionally until the tower is covered by the circle of undistorted projection, while center and vanishing points remain unchanged.

In a case like this, the *Perspective Construction Sheet* (P.C. sheet) described in Chap. 1, Method 7 can ease the proper selection of the station point. This example has been shown to bring this condition to the designer's attention. It requires particular care in the selection of the sector of view and in the determination of the margin m. To avoid the distortion of the upper part of the tower, a margin of at least 60 ft should have been added to the height H_o of the object; i.e.,

$$H_o + m - \tfrac{1}{2}d_H = H_p$$

(see PREPARATION OF THE SITE PLAN, step 2, page 36).

CONCLUSION: As a high object moves closer to the sidelines of the perspective, the chord of the circle of undistorted projection decreases, consequently the factor m must be increased.

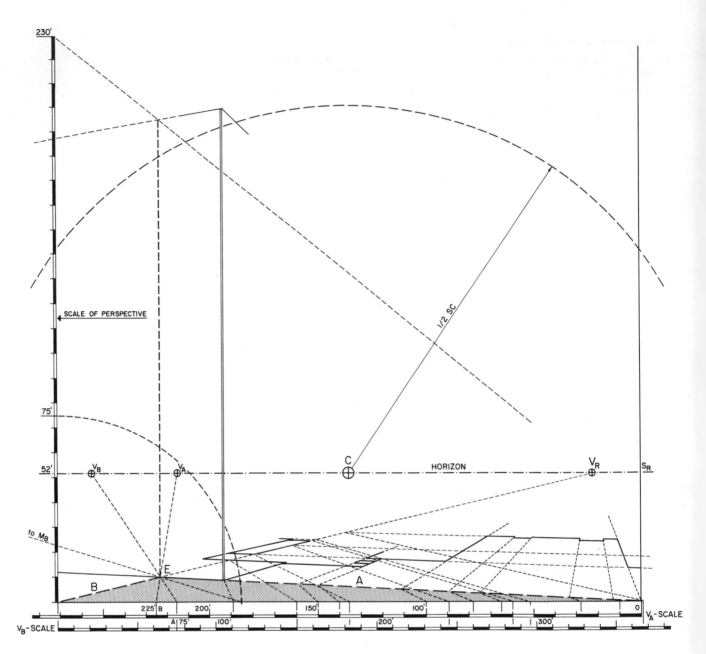

Fig. 1, 3b-9

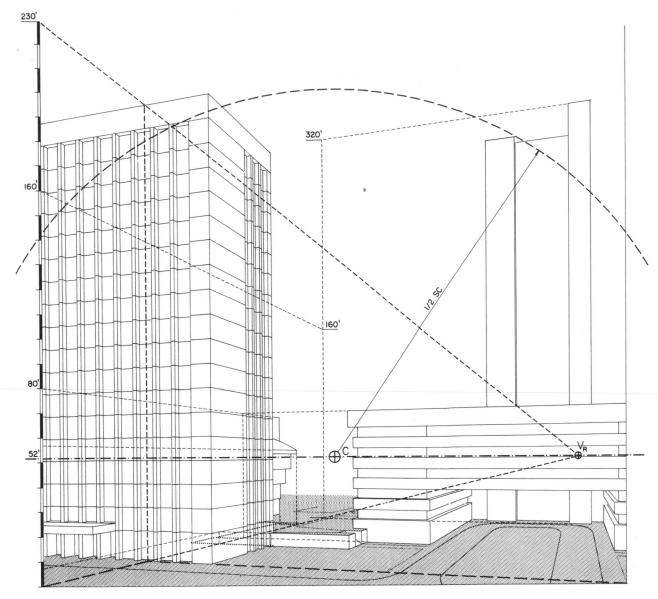

Fig. 1, 3b-10

METHOD 4:   45° Perspective

Characteristics

The rectangle AB is positioned to the picture plane at 45°.

The central line of vision SC bisects the total span $V_L V_R = T$ in C.

The maximal width P_{max} of the perspective equals the distance SC from the station point S to the center C of the perspective; i.e.,

$$P_{max} = SC$$

SC as the height of the triangle $V_L S V_R$ upon its hypotenuse T equals $T/2$, i.e.,

$$SC = \tfrac{1}{2} T$$

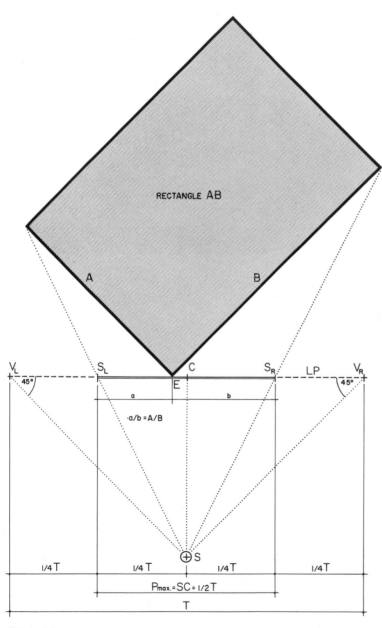

RECTANGLE AB

Fig. 1, 4-1

This is the most economical result of any method described except the central perspective. All other methods offer less than $\frac{1}{2}T$.

The distance from the left vanishing point V_L to C equals the distance from the right vanishing point V_R to C, or

$$V_L C = C V_R$$

The height H_o of the object at its point of intersection with the picture plane has to be equal to or less than $\frac{3}{4}P_{max}$, i.e.,

$$H_o = H_p \leq \frac{3}{4}P_{max}$$

The point of contact of AB at the picture plane is E.

The projection $a = S_L E$ of the rectangle's left side A upon the picture plane is to the projection $b = E S_R$ of the right side B as $A:B$; i.e.,

$$a:b = A:B$$

Consequently

$$a = S_L E = \frac{A}{A+B} P_{max}$$

This formula locates the point E where the object touches the picture plane.

Applicability

The 45° perspective construction is one of the easiest methods for illustrating an object. It is particularly useful for objects with a rectangular floor plan; i.e., where one side should be considerably longer than the other. A square object projected by this method appears less interesting because it is centered in the perspective and its sides A and B are equally long, which does not enhance the appearance of the perspective.

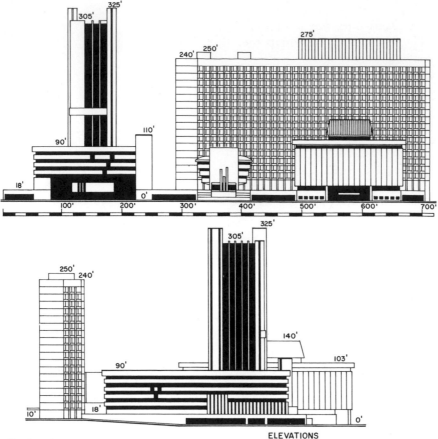

Fig. 1, 4-2

ELEVATIONS

Preparation of the Site Plan

1. Enclose that part of the object to be illustrated by drawing the rectangle AB; then measure its sides A and B in any scale in order to obtain the ratio $A:B$, provided that A and B are measured in the same scale. In this demonstration the ratio is $A:B = 400':560' = 5:7$.

2. To obtain accurate information concerning the use of the P_{max} projection or the P_H projection (see Chap. 3, Method 6), draw in the site plan the line LP through the foremost corner E_o of AB under an angle of 45° and drop perpendiculars d_A and d_B upon LP (see Fig. 1, 4-3). The distance between d_A and d_B is W_o. To the scale of the site plan scale off $d_A = 280$ ft, $d_B = 396$ ft, and $W_o = 676$ ft. Deduct $\frac{1}{2}(d_A + d_B)$ from W_o to obtain $P_{o,max}$:

$$P_{o,max} = W_o - \tfrac{1}{2}(d_A + d_B) = 676' - \tfrac{1}{2}(280' + 396')$$
$$= 338'$$

Mark the highest point of the object X, scale off to the scale of the site plan the right angular distance d_H between X and LP, and deduct one-half of it from H_o, the height of the object at X, i.e.,

$$H_o - \tfrac{1}{2}d_H = 325' - \tfrac{1}{2} \times 180' = 235' = H_p$$

H_p is the projected height upon the picture plane. Determine the height of the horizon H_H, keeping in mind that it should not exceed one-third H_p:

$$\tfrac{1}{3}H_p = \tfrac{1}{3} \times 235' \approx 78'$$

Deduct H_H from H_p to obtain one-half SC_o:

$$\tfrac{1}{2}SC_o = H_p - H_H = 235' - 78' = 157'$$
$$SC_o = 314'$$

SC_o is the distance between C_o, the center of $P_{o,\text{max}}$, and the station point S on the site plan.

CONCLUSION: SC_o is less than $P_{o,\text{max}}$; therefore the construction of the perspective has to be continued according to the P_{max} projection. If SC_o exceeds $P_{o,\text{max}}$, then the P_H projection must be applied.

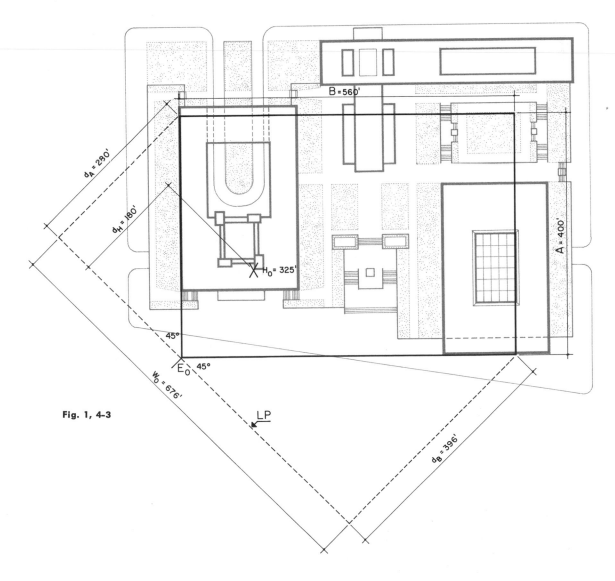

Fig. 1, 4–3

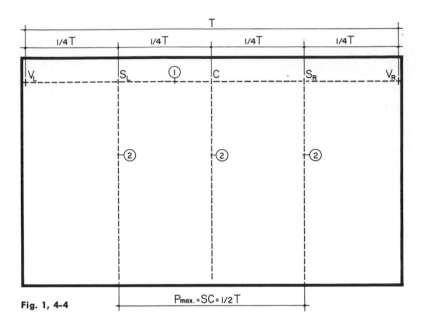

Fig. 1, 4-4

$P_{\max}$: the Maximal Size of the Perspective

$P_{\max} = \frac{1}{2}T$: the maximal width $P_{\max}$ equals one-half the table length T. It should not exceed 30 in. for reasons of convenience, because the construction of a 30-in.-wide perspective already requires in this case a 60-in.-long drawing board and a straight edge of at least 50 in.

1. Draw a temporary horizon on the upper part of the drawing board and locate the vanishing points V_L and V_R.
2. Divide the distance T between V_L and V_R in four equal parts and drop perpendiculars S_L at the first quarter from the left, C at the second quarter, and S_R at the third quarter. $S_L S_R$ is the maximal length $P_{\max}$ and measures $\frac{1}{2}T$. From here follow the instructions for DETERMINATION OF THE LOCATION OF POINT E.

P_H: the Maximal Width of the Perspective for High Objects

1. Draw a temporary horizon on the upper part of the drawing board and locate the two vanishing points V_L and V_R.
2. Bisect the distance T between V_L and V_R in order to locate the center C of the perspective.
3. Derive P_H by the formula

$$P_H = \frac{W_o}{d_A + 2SC_o + d_B}\, T$$

The dimensions of W_o, d_A, and d_B have to be scaled off on the prepared site plan (see Fig. 1, 4-3). SC_o is obtained as de-

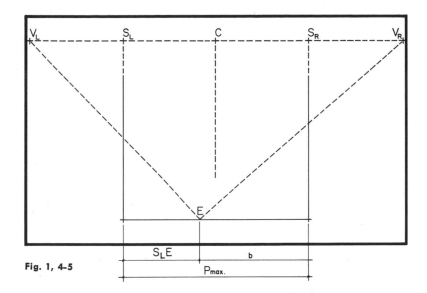

Fig. 1, 4-5

scribed in PREPARATION OF THE SITE PLAN. Lay off $\frac{1}{2}P_H$ to the left and to the right of C, locating the sidelines S_L and S_R. Drop perpendiculars from S_L and S_R and continue according to DETERMINATION OF THE LOCATION OF POINT E.

Determination of the Location of Point E

(For graphical solution see Chap. 3, Method 7.)

To construct the perspective in accordance with the proportions of the rectangle AB and its position to the picture plane, it is essential to determine properly E, the point at which the nearest corner of the rectangle touches the picture plane.

Locate point E by employing the formula

$$S_L E = \frac{A}{A + B} P_{\max} \text{ or } P_H$$

Final Adjustment of the Horizon

Since the size of the perspective was determined by the size of the available drawing board or was chosen by the designer, it has no relation to the object as far as the scale is concerned. However, to establish the height of the object in this perspective, it is necessary to know its scale. Use one of the solutions in Chap. 3, Method 4 (*a*, *b*, or *c*) for converting a perspective line into its true length in any perspective. Having thus obtained one true length of either side of AB, the designer is able to scale off with this side the respective height of the object upon the picture plane and to set the final horizon accordingly.

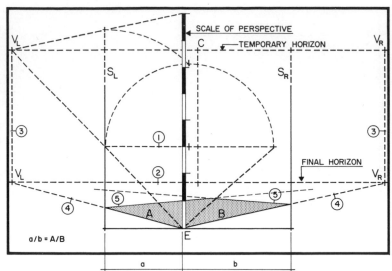

Fig. 1, 4-6

1. Draw the horizontal through the intersection of EV_L and S_L and continue according to Chap. 3, Method 4, Solution c, thus obtaining the respective length of A upon the vertical at E.

2. Keeping in mind that the maximal height of the horizon should not exceed $\frac{1}{4}P_{max} = \frac{1}{8}T$, locate the horizon in this range, measured from the groundline of the perspective. In this demonstration the range is 85 ft (see Fig. 1, 4-8).

3. Draw the final horizon all the way across the drawing board and transfer temporary V_L and V_R by dropping perpendiculars from the temporary horizon.

4. Draw perspective lines from E to V_L and V_R on the final horizon.

5. Complete the perspective of AB by drawing perspective lines from S_L to V_R and from S_R to V_L.

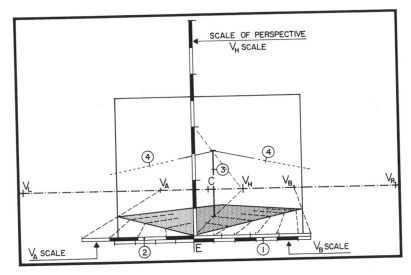

Fig. 1, 4-7

Completion of the Perspective

1. Beginning at E on the groundline, lay off the diverse sections of side B to the right in any suitable scale and continue according to Chap. 3, Method 2 or 3 (see perspective Fig. 1, 4-8).

2. Repeat every step to the left of E in order to locate the perspectively reduced sections of side A.

3. Erect verticals at the points of all corners of the object; then transfer appropriate heights from E by employing Method 5 in Chap. 3.

4. Complete the picture by drawing perspective lines from the heights of the object (see perspective Fig. 1, 4-8).

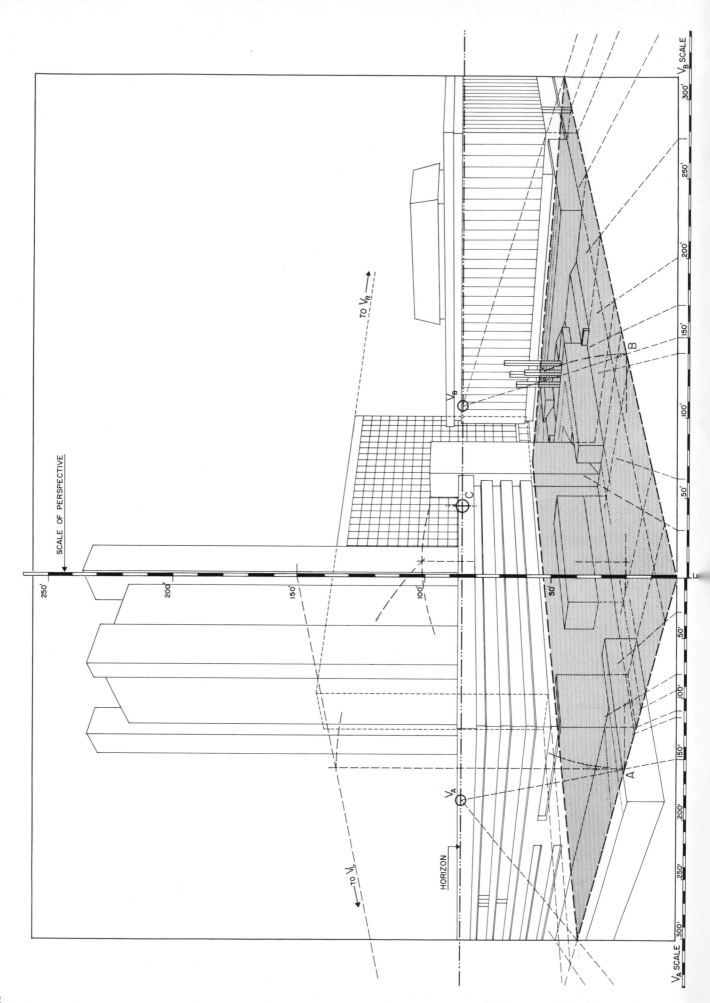

SCALE OF PERSPECTIVE

TO V$_R$ →

V$_B$

C

B

SCALE OF PERSPECTIVE

250'
200'
150'
100'
50'

← TO V$_L$

HORIZON

V$_A$

A

V$_A$ SCALE   300'   250'   200'   150'   100'   50'   50'   100'   150'   200'   250'   300'   V$_B$ SCALE

METHOD 5: 30°/60° Perspective

Characteristics

The rectangle AB is positioned to the picture plane LP at an angle of 30°/60° (see Fig. 1, 5-1). The central line of vision intersects the total span $V_LV_R = T$ at C, located $\frac{1}{4}T$ from V_L or V_R.

The maximal width P_{max} of the perspective equals the distance SC between the center of the perspective C and the station point S. It is determined by the formula

$$P_{max} = SC = \tfrac{1}{4}T\sqrt{3} = 0.43\ T$$

The distance between the left vanishing point V_L and C and the distance between C and the right vanishing point V_R are either

$$V_LC = \tfrac{1}{4}T \qquad \text{and} \qquad CV_R = \tfrac{3}{4}T$$

or

$$V_LC = \tfrac{3}{4}T \qquad \text{and} \qquad CV_R = \tfrac{1}{4}T$$

depending upon the location of the 30°/60° angle.

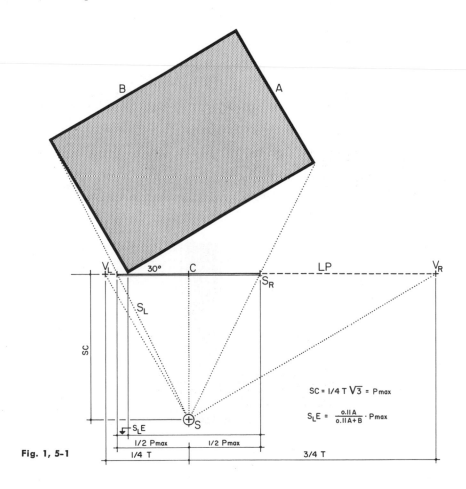

Fig. 1, 5-1

The height H_o of the object at its intersection with the picture plane LP has to be equal to or less than $\frac{3}{4}P_{max}$:

$$H_o = H_p \leq \frac{3}{4}P_{max}$$

The point of contact of AB and LP is E. It is located by the formula

$$S_L E = \frac{0.11A}{0.11A + B} P_{max}$$

For the graphical determination of the location of E see Chap. 3, Method 7.

Applicability

The 30°/60° perspective construction was always and still is an easy way to illustrate any object. It is particularly useful for objects with a square or almost square floor plan and with one main elevation, yet it gives an idea of the depth of the object. Extremely long objects, too, whose length should be subdued, can be arranged in an interesting perspective.

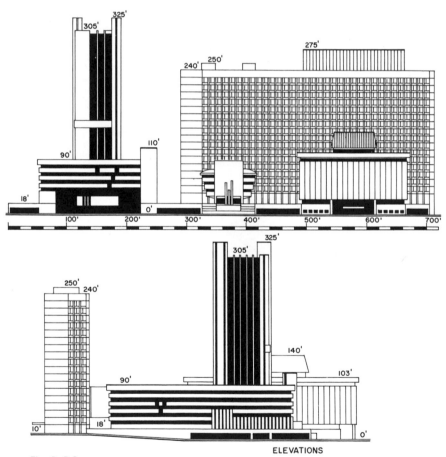

ELEVATIONS

Fig. 1, 5-2

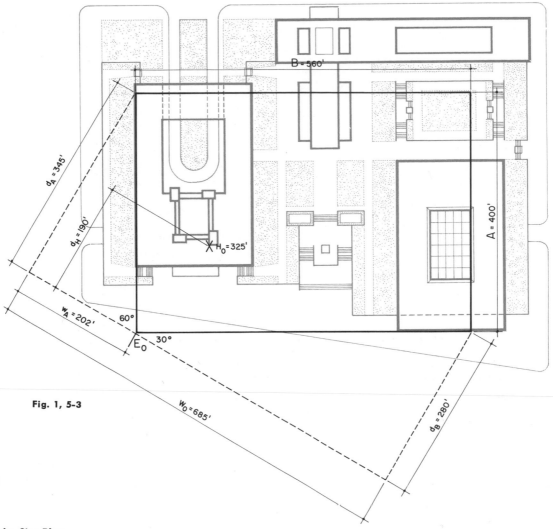

Fig. 1, 5-3

Preparation of the Site Plan

1. Enclose that part of the object to be illustrated by the rectangle AB (see Fig. 1, 5-3); then measure its sides A and B in any scale in order to obtain the ratio $A:B = 400':560' = 5:7$.

2. To obtain accurate information concerning whether the P_{max} projection or the P_H projection should be used, draw in the site plan the line LP through the foremost corner E_o of AB at a 60°/30° angle and drop the perpendiculars d_A and d_B upon LP. The distance between d_A and d_B is W_o. To the scale of the site plan scale off $d_A = 345$ ft, $d_B = 280$ ft, and $W_o = 685$ ft. Deduct $\frac{1}{2}(d_A + d_B)$ from W_o to obtain $P_{o,max}$.

$$P_{o,max} = W_o - \frac{1}{2}(d_A + d_B) = 685' - \frac{1}{2}(345' + 280')$$
$$= 372.5'$$

Mark the highest point of the object X, scale off to the scale of the site plan the rectangular distance d_H between X and LP, and deduct one-half of it from the height of the object at X; i.e.,

$$H_P = H_o - \tfrac{1}{2}d_H = 325' - \tfrac{1}{2} \times 190' = 230'$$

H_p is the projected height upon the picture plane. Determine the height of the horizon H_H, keeping in mind that it should not exceed one-third H_P:

$$\tfrac{1}{3}H_P = \tfrac{1}{3} \times 230' = 77'$$

Deduct H_H from H_P to obtain $\tfrac{1}{2}SC_o$:

$$\tfrac{1}{2}SC_o = H_P - H_H = 230' - 77' = 153'$$
$$SC_o = 306'$$

SC_o is the distance between C_o, the center of $P_{o,max}$, and the station point S on the site plan.

CONCLUSION: SC_o is less than $P_{o,max}$. The construction of the perspective must therefore be continued according to the P_{max} projection. If SC_o exceeds $P_{o,max}$, then the P_H projection must be applied.

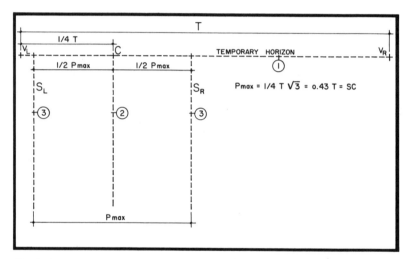

Fig. 1, 5-4

P_{max}: the Maximal Size of the Perspective

$$P_{max} = 0.43\,T$$

In this demonstration the span from V_L to V_R measures 60 in., hence the width of the perspective will be

$$0.43 \times 60'' = 26''$$

Compare with Method 4 (page 48).

1. Draw a temporary horizon on the upper part of the drawing board and locate the vanishing points V_L and V_R (see Fig. 1, 5-4).
2. Divide the distance T between V_L and V_R into four equal parts. Mark the first part C—from the left in this demonstration. Drop the perpendicular from C.
3. Lay off $\frac{1}{2}P_{max} = \frac{1}{2} \times 26$ in. $= 13$ in. to the left and to the right of C in order to locate S_L and S_R. Drop perpendiculars, which mark the left and right sides of the perspective.

P_H: the Maximal Width of the Perspective for High Objects

1. Draw a temporary horizon on the upper part of the drawing board and locate the two vanishing points V_L and V_R.
2. Divide the distance T between V_L and V_R into four equal parts; mark the first part C, from V_L in this demonstration; and drop the perpendicular from C.
3. Derive P_H by the formula

$$\tfrac{1}{2}P_H = \frac{W_o}{d_A + 2SC_o + d_B}\,SC$$

The dimensions of W_o, d_A, and d_B have to be scaled off on the prepared site plan (see Fig. 1, 5-3). SC_o is obtained as described under PREPARATION OF THE SITE PLAN.

4. Lay off $\frac{1}{2}P_H$ to the left and to the right of C, marking S_L and S_R, and drop perpendiculars. From here follow the instructions for DETERMINATION OF THE LOCATION OF POINT E, P_H section.

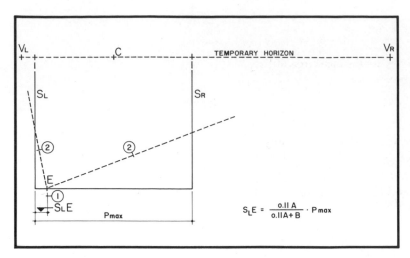

Fig. 1, 5-5

Determination of the Location of Point *E*

(For graphical solution see Chap. 3, Method 7.)

To construct the perspective in accordance with the proportion of the rectangle *AB* and its position to the picture plane, it is essential to determine properly *E*, the point at which the nearest corner of the rectangle touches the picture plane.

1. Draw the horizontal *G* on the lower part of the drawing board, thereby connecting S_L and S_R (see Fig. 1, 5-5). In order to locate *E*, derive $S_L E$ by the formula

$$S_L E = \frac{0.11A}{0.11A + B} P_{\max} = \frac{0.11 \times 400'}{0.11 \times 400' + 560'} 26''$$

$$= \frac{44}{604} 26'' \approx 1.9''$$

   Lay off $S_L E$ from S_L to the right and mark it *E*.

2. Draw perspective lines from *E* to V_L and V_R, intersecting S_L and S_R.

P_H *section:* To derive $S_L E$ of a P_H projection, apply the following formula:

$$S_L E = \frac{(A/B)(d_A/w_A)(V_L S_L/S_R V_R)}{[(A/B)(d_A/w_A)(V_L S_L/S_R V_R)] + 1} P_H$$

d_A and w_A must be scaled off in the prepared site plan (see Fig. 1, 5-3), whereas $V_L S_L$, $S_R V_R$, and P_H have to be scaled off in the perspective.

Final Adjustment of the Horizon

Since the size of the perspective was determined by the size of the available drawing board or was chosen by the designer, it has no relation to the object as far as the scale is concerned. However, in order to establish the height of the object in the perspective, it is necessary to know its scale. Use one of the three solutions in Chap. 3, Method 4 (*a*, *b*, or *c*), for converting a perspective line into its true length. Having thus obtained one proper length of either side of *AB*, the designer is able to scale off with this side the respective height of the object upon the picture plane and to set the final horizon accordingly.

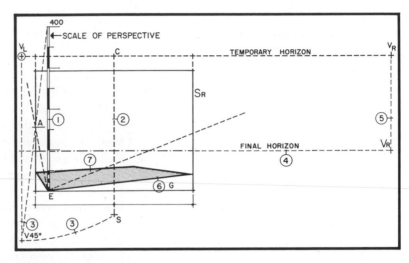

Fig. 1, 5-6

1. Erect a vertical at *E*.
2. Lay off $SC = 26$ in. from *C* downward to locate *S* on the perpendicular at *C*.
3. Drop a perpendicular from V_L and rotate *S* from V_L downward to locate V_{45} upon the perpendicular. Follow the instructions in Chap. 3, Method 4, Solution *b*, thus projecting the equivalent length of *A* upon the vertical at *E*. Calibrate the vertical at *E* to 400 units ($A = 400$ ft), or whatever appears to be convenient as the respective scale of the perspective.
4. Draw the final horizon above *G* approximately one-third of the height of the perspective.
5. Transfer the temporary V_L and V_R to the final horizon by dropping perpendiculars.
6. Draw perspective lines from *E* to V_L and V_R on the final horizon.
7. Complete the perspective of *AB* by drawing perspective lines from S_L to V_R and from S_R to V_L.

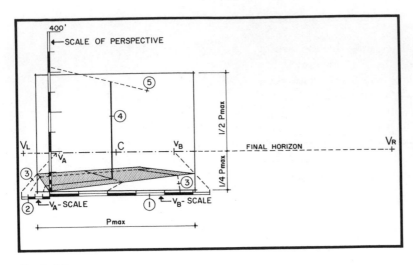

Fig. 1, 5-7

The Completion of the Perspective

1. Beginning at *E*, lay off the diverse sections of side *B* to the right in any suitable scale and continue according to Chap. 3, Method 2, in order to project these sections upon EV_R.

2. Repeat every step to the left of *E* in order to locate the perspectively reduced sections of side *A* upon EV_L (see perspective Fig. 1, 5-8).

3. Draw perspective lines from sections of EV_L to V_R and from EV_R to V_L in order to locate the corners of the object.

4. Erect verticals at every point of all corners of the object; then transfer the respective heights from the scale at *E*, following the instructions in Chap. 3, Method 5 (see perspective Fig. 1, 5-9).

5. Complete the perspective by drawing perspective lines from various heights of the object to the respective vanishing points.

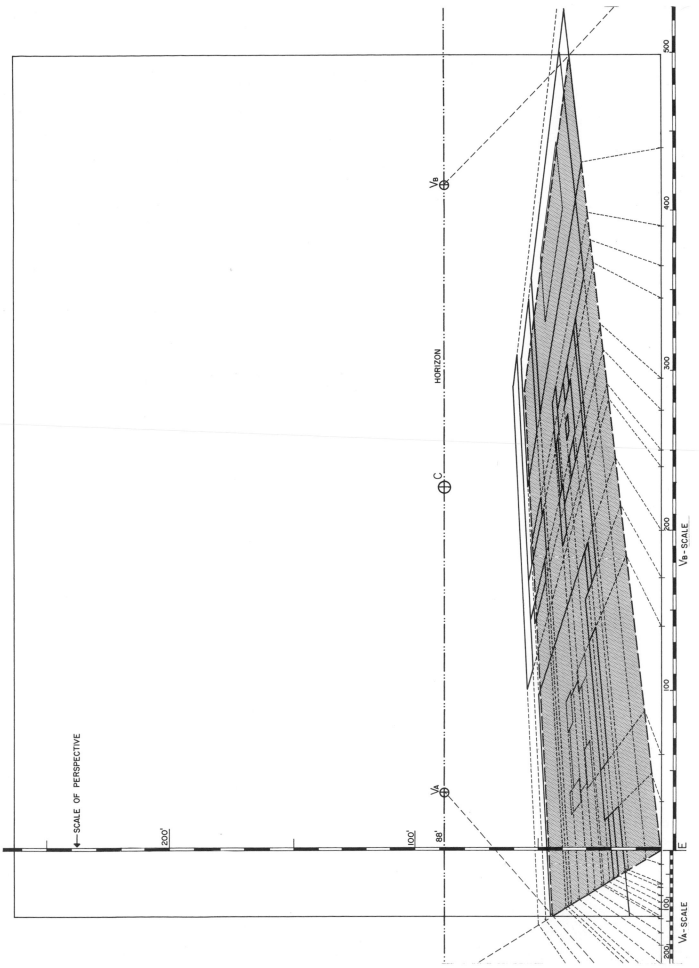

SCALE OF PERSPECTIVE

200'

100'

88'

HORIZON

V_B

C

V_A

V_B-SCALE

V_A-SCALE

E

100

200

300

400

500

100

200

Fig. 1, 5-8

61

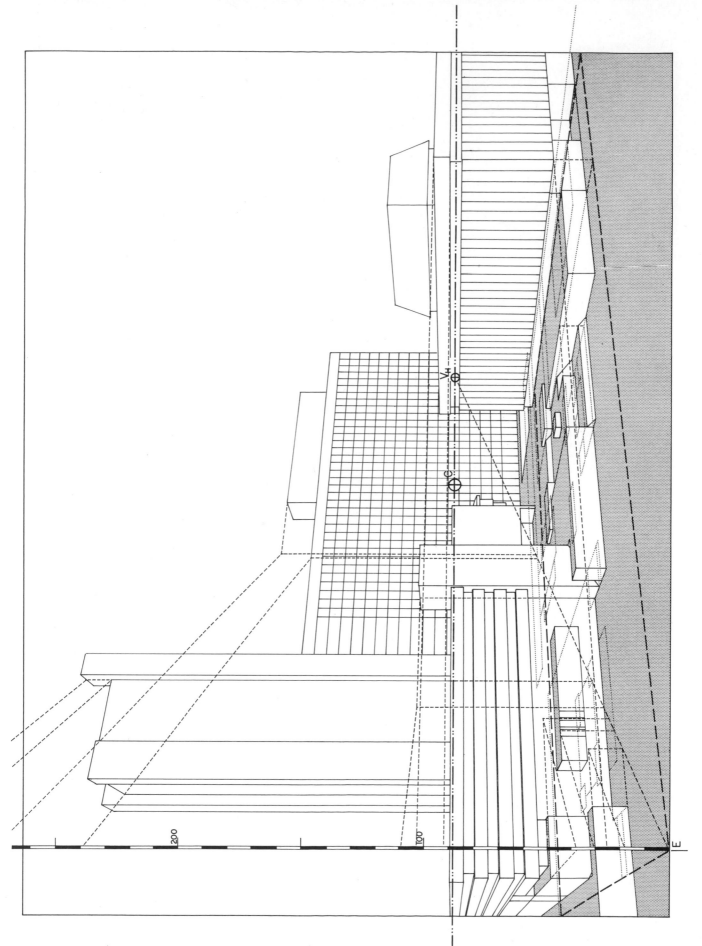

Fig. 1, 5-9

METHOD 6: Angle of Position Chosen by the Designer

Characteristics

The position of the object AB to the picture plane is chosen by the designer; i.e., the angle of position is not determined by the method itself as in the 45° and 30°/60° perspectives. Any data necessary for the projection must be obtained from the position on the site plan (see Fig. 1, 6-1). A certain limitation has to be considered: the two angles of the position α and β must range between 63.5° and 26.5°. If this range is neglected, only one side of AB appears on the picture plane. Bird's-eye perspectives are not affected by this condition.

Applicability

This method can be used to illustrate any object. It has the significant advantage that the designer is able to choose any position under which he wants to view the object.

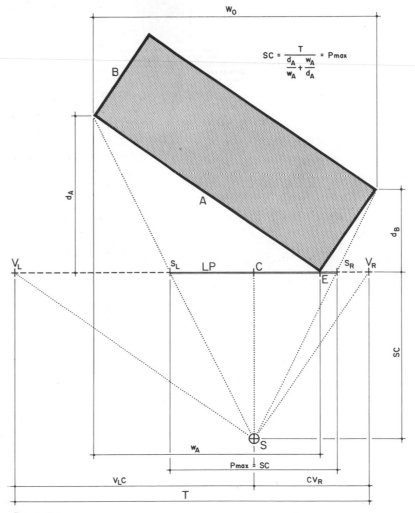

Fig. 1, 6-1

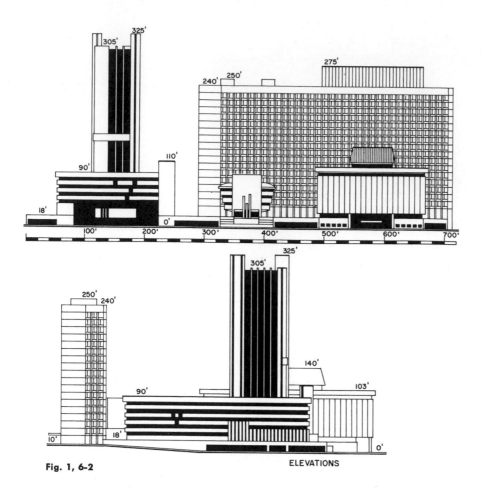

Fig. 1, 6-2   ELEVATIONS

Preparation of the Site Plan

Prepare the site plan by following the instructions in Chap. 3, Method 6 (see Fig. 1, 6-3 and 6-3a).

1. Enclose that part of the object to be illustrated by the rectangle AB and measure its sides A and B in any scale in order to obtain the ratio $A:B = 300':108' = 2.78$.

2. Draw through the foremost corner E_o the straight line LP to establish the angle of position under which the object is to be seen.

3. Drop the perpendiculars d_A and d_B from the left and right corners of AB upon LP. The distance W_o between d_A and d_B measured to the scale of the site plan $= 306$ ft, $d_A = 170$ ft, and $d_B = 90$ ft.

4. Mark the highest point of the object X with the height $H_o =$ 320 ft. Deduct one-half of the distance between X and LP from H_o to obtain the projected height H_P of the object upon the picture plane.

$$H_P = H_o - \tfrac{1}{2}d_H = 320' - \tfrac{1}{2} \times 250' = 195'$$

Determine the height of the horizon H_H, which should not exceed $\tfrac{1}{3}H_P = {}^{195}\!/_{3} = 65$ ft. Deduct H_H from H_P in order to obtain $\tfrac{1}{2}SC_o$, which is one-half of the distance between LP and the mathematical station point S on the site plan, i.e.,

$$\tfrac{1}{2}SC_o = H_P - H_H = 195' - 65' = 130'$$
$$SC_o = 260'$$

Note: Although SC_o and SC do not appear in the construction of the perspective, their value is necessary to determine the size of the perspective and the vanishing points.

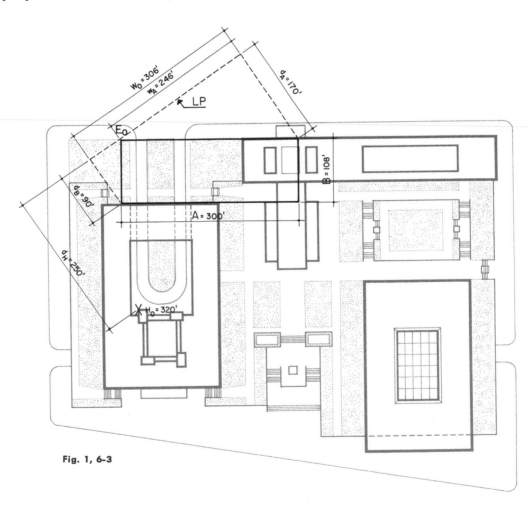

Fig. 1, 6-3

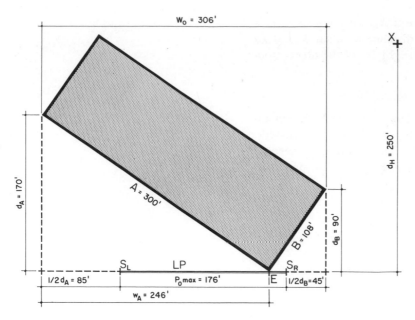

Fig. 1, 6-3a

5. Deduct $\frac{1}{2}(d_A + d_B)$ from the width of the object W_o to obtain the maximum width $P_{o,\max}$ on the site plan.

$$W_o - \frac{1}{2}(d_A + d_B) = 306' - \frac{1}{2}(170' + 90')$$
$$= 306' - 130' = 176' = P_{o,\max}$$

(See Fig. 1, 6-3a.)

CONCLUSION: SC_o exceeds $P_{o,\max}$ by more than 10 percent; therefore the perspective has to be constructed according to Chap. 3, Method 6, in order to avoid obvious distortions in the upper part of the perspective. See P_H: THE MAXIMAL WIDTH OF THE PERSPECTIVE FOR HIGH OBJECTS.

$P_{\max}$: the Maximal Size of the Perspective

Provided that the height of the object does not exceed the circle of undistorted projection, i.e.,

$$SC_o \leq P_{o,\max}$$

SC is determined by the position of AB to the line of the picture plane LP and the total span T on the drawing board.

$$T = V_L C + C V_R$$

Bringing these factors into relation results in the formula

$$P_{\max} = SC = \frac{T}{(w_A/d_A + d_A/w_A)} \quad \text{or} \quad P_{\max} = \frac{T}{\tan \alpha + \tan \beta}$$

T must be measured in inches on the drawing board; the data in parentheses can be measured to any scale on the site plan. Hence, the amount of SC and $P_{\max}$ results in inches.

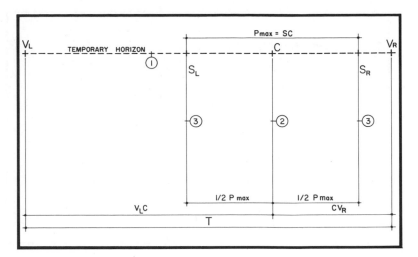

Fig. 1, 6-4

1. Draw a temporary horizon on the upper part of the drawing board and mark the ends V_L and V_R.

   $$V_L V_R = T$$

2. Calculate $V_L C$ to establish C by employing the formulas

   $$SC = \frac{T}{d_A/w_A + w_A/d_A} = P_{\max}$$

   $$V_L C = \frac{w_A}{d_A} SC$$

   $V_L C$ has to be measured from V_L to the right, thereby locating C.

3. Lay off $\frac{1}{2} P_{\max}$ to the left of C and $\frac{1}{2} P_{\max}$ to the right, thereby locating S_L and S_R. Then drop perpendiculars as the left and right sidelines of the perspective.

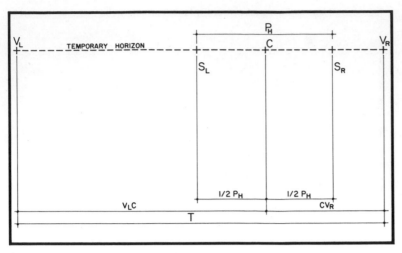

Fig. 1, 6-5

P_H: **the Maximal Width of the Perspective for High Objects**

1. Draw a temporary horizon at a convenient height across the drawing board and locate the vanishing points V_L and V_R. Scale off in inches the distance T between V_L and V_R. In this demonstration $T = 60$ in.

 Derive SC by the formula

$$SC = \frac{T}{w_A/d_A + d_A/w_A} = \frac{60''}{246'/170' + 170'/246'}$$
$$= \frac{60''}{1.45 + 0.69} = 28''$$

 $\frac{1}{2}SC = 14$ in. represents the radius of the circle of undistorted projection.

2. Locate the center C of the perspective by employing the formulas

$$V_LC = \frac{w_A}{d_A} SC = 1.45 \times 28'' = 40.6''$$

$$CV_R = \frac{d_A}{w_A} SC = 0.69 \times 28'' = 19.4''$$

3. Derive the maximal width P_H of the perspective by employing the formula

$$\frac{1}{2}P_H = \frac{W_o}{d_A + 2SC_o + d_B} SC$$
$$\frac{1}{2}P_H = \frac{306'}{170' + (2 \times 260') + 90'} 28''$$
$$= 0.392 \times 28'' = 11''$$

Lay off $\frac{1}{2}P_H$ to the left and to the right of C, locating S_L and S_R. Erect verticals, which are the sidelines of the perspective. The distance between S_L and S_R is $P_H = 22$ in.

Determination of the Location of Point *E*

(For graphical solution see Chap. 3, Method 7.)

To construct the perspective in accordance with the proportions of the rectangle AB and its position to the picture plane, it is essential to determine properly E, i.e., the point at which the nearest corner of the rectangle touches the picture plane. See Figs. 1, 6-1, 6-3, and 6-3*a*.

1. Locate point E by the formula in Chap. 3, Method 7.
   For P_{max}:

$$S_L E = \frac{(A/B)(d_A/w_A)(V_L S_L/S_R V_R)}{[(A/B)(d_A/w_A)(V_L S_L/S_R V_R)] + 1} P_{max}$$

For P_H:

$$S_L E = \frac{(2.78)(0.69)(3.52)}{[(2.78)(0.69)(3.52)] + 1} P_H = \frac{6.8}{7.8} 22'' = 19.15''$$

Drop a perpendicular at E.

2. Draw the groundline G on the lower part of the drawing board from perpendicular S_L to S_R, intersecting the perpendicular at E.
3. Draw perspective lines from the intersection at E to V_L and V_R in order to intersect S_L and S_R.

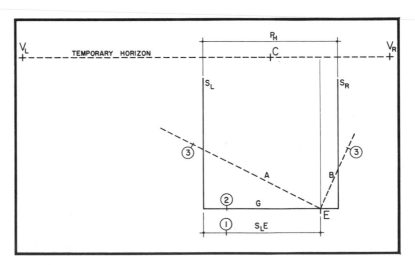

Fig. 1, 6-6

Final Adjustment of the Horizon

Since the size of the perspective was related to the available drawing board or chosen by the designer, its scale has to be derived from the construction of the perspective itself. The solutions in Chap. 3, Method 4 demonstrate the conversion of a perspective line into its proper length. Having one true dimension projected upon the picture plane, the respective height of the object can be scaled off and the final horizon set accordingly.

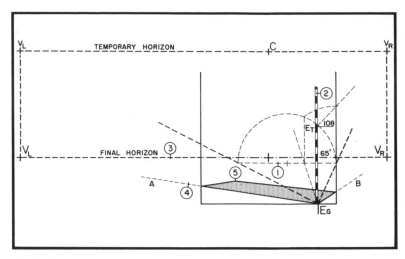

Fig. 1, 6-7

1. See Fig. 1, 6-7 and Method 4, Solution c in Chap. 3. Draw a horizontal from the intersection of the perspective line $E_G V_R$ and S_R to the left in order to intersect the perspective line $V_L E_G$. Draw a semicircle over this horizontal limited by $V_L E_G$ and S_R.

Draw the connecting line from E_G to C in order to intersect the horizontal. Erect the vertical at this intersection in order to intersect the semicircle. Rotate the intersection of the semicircle from the intersection $E_G V_R$ and S_R to intersect S_R. Draw a perspective line from V_R through this intersection and continue to locate E_T at vertical E.

The distance between E_G and E_T is the true length of B upon the picture plane.

2. Divide the vertical $E_G E_T$ according to the measurement of $B = 108$ ft in the site plan. It can now be used as the specific scale for the diverse heights of this perspective.

3. Draw final horizon $= 65$ ft above G according to this scale; or, in case of the P_{max} projection, not more than $\frac{1}{4} P_{max}$ above G.

4. Draw perspective lines from E_G to V_L and V_R.

5. Complete the perspective layout of AB by drawing perspective lines from S_L to V_R and from S_R to V_L.

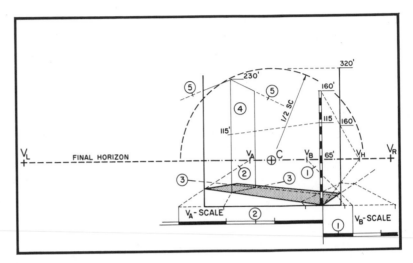

Fig. 1, 6–8

Completion of the Perspective

1. Beginning at E, lay off the diverse sections of side B to the right in any suitable scale and continue according to Chap. 3, Method 2, in order to project these sections upon EV_R.

2. Repeat every step to the left of E in order to project the sections of A upon EV_L (see perspective Fig. 1, 6-9).

3. Draw perspective lines from the sections of A to V_R and from B to V_L in order to locate the corners of the object (see Fig. 1, 6-8 and perspective Fig. 1, 6-9).

4. Erect verticals at every point of all corners of the object and transfer the respective heights from the scale at E according to Chap. 3, Method 5.

5. Complete the perspective by drawing the perspective lines from various heights of the object to the respective vanishing points (see perspective Fig. 1, 6-10). The corners of the main parts have been established. Now continue with the projection of the intermediate parts separately in accordance with Method 2 in Chap. 3 (see perspective Fig. 1, 6-10).

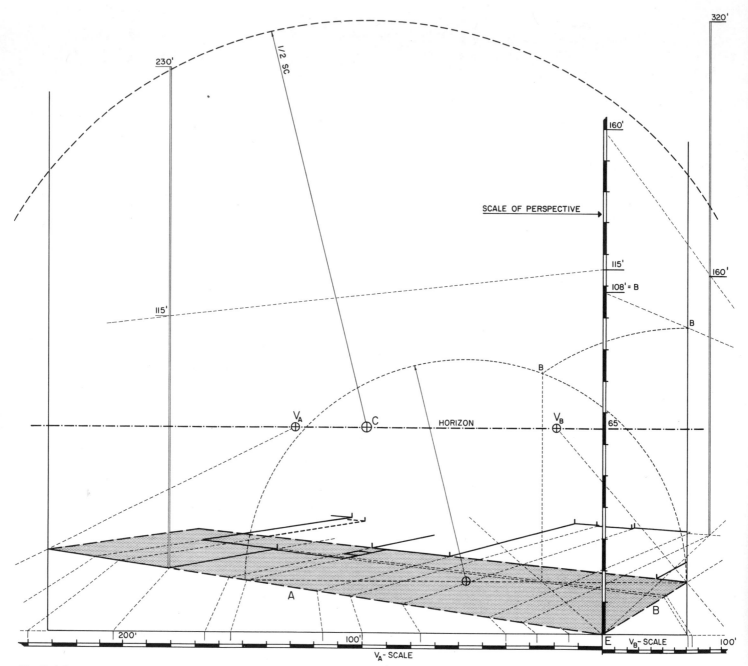

Fig. 1, 6-9

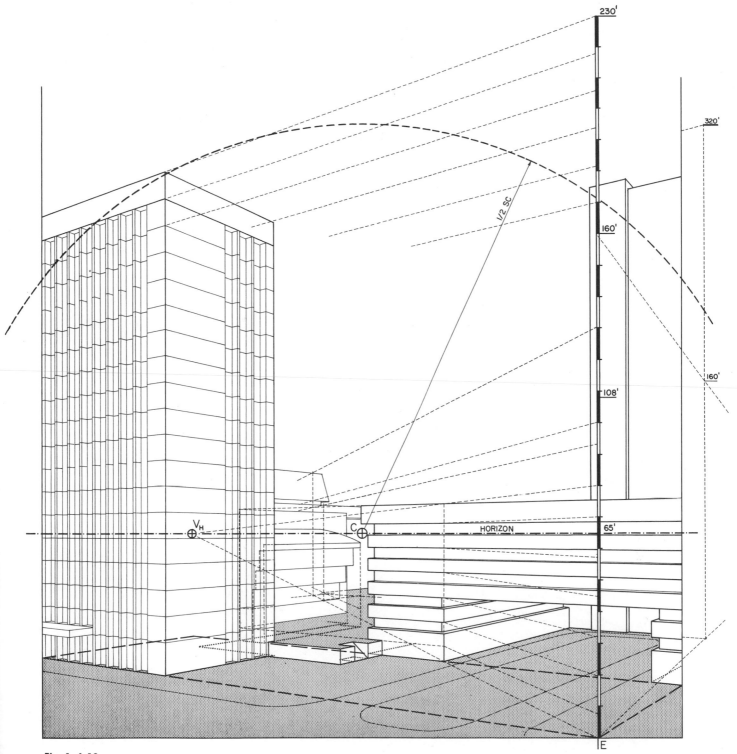

Fig. 1, 6-10

230'

320'

160'

1/2 SC

160'

108'

V_H

C

HORIZON

65'

E

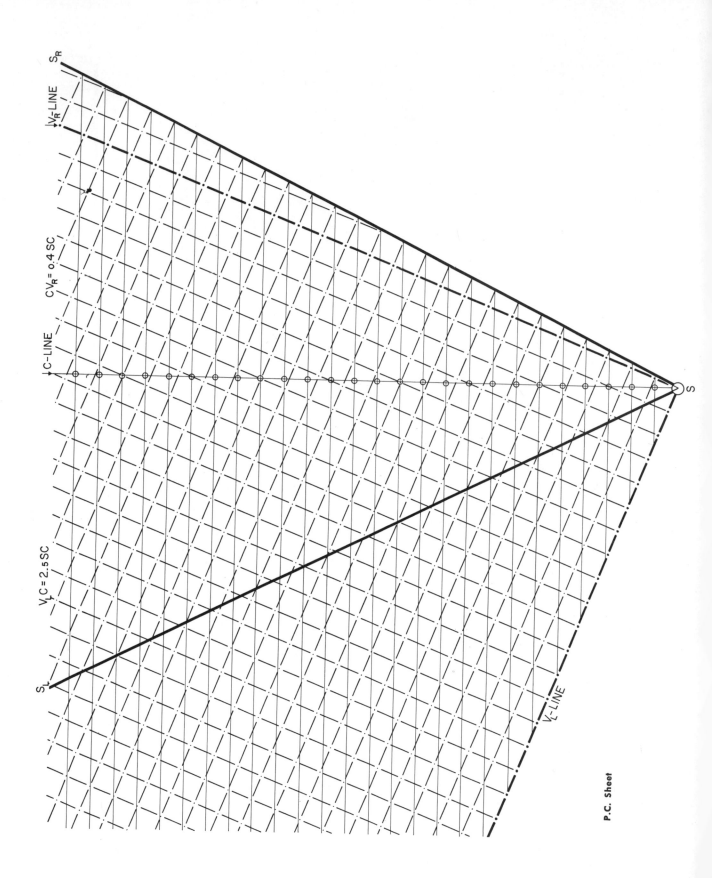

P.C. Sheet

METHOD 7: Application of the Perspective Construction Sheet

See opposite illustration of the P.C. sheet.

Characteristics

The Perspective Construction sheet method is a variation of the central perspective, except that it has two vanishing points. It has been especially developed for a wider use of the central perspective, but it can also be employed with the methods previously described. By applying the P.C. sheet, the designer can easily find and establish the sector of the view anticipated.

The rectangle AB is positioned to the picture plane as follows:

The distances between vanishing points and the center of the perspective C are $0.4SC$ and $2.5SC$, respectively. This locates one vanishing point in the perspective picture, so that the object is slightly tilted either to the right or to the left vanishing point.

The maximal width P_{max} of the perspective equals SC, the distance between the station point S and the center C of the perspective. P_{max} is $\frac{1}{3}T$. In the P.C. sheet method T represents the distance from one of the vanishing points V_L or V_R to C plus $\frac{1}{2}P_{max}$.

The height H_o of the object at its intersection with the picture plane has to be equal to or less than $\frac{3}{4}P_{max}$.

The point E at which the rectangle AB touches the picture plane coincides either with the left side S_L of the perspective picture or with the right side S_R.

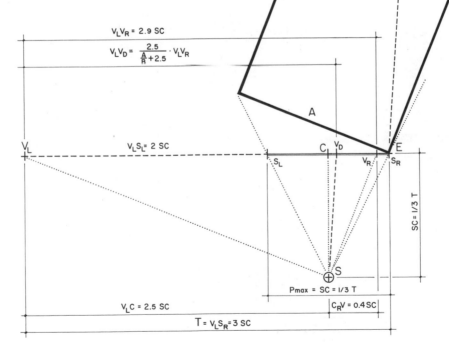

Fig. 1, 7-1

Applicability

Perspectives of streets, corridors, malls, plazas, halls, bridges, and interiors in general, as long as an eye level not higher than $\frac{3}{4}P_{max}$ is used. The method cannot be applied to bird's-eye perspectives.

Preparation of the Site Plan

1. Place the P.C. sheet over the site plan in such a way that the point S at the intersection of S_L and S_R approximately locates the station point from which the designer wants the object to be seen. Then set the dash-point-dash grid parallel with the sides of the object and fasten the P.C. sheet in this position.

2. Cover the site plan and the P.C. sheet with transparent paper for an auxiliary construction. Mark the highest and nearest point on the object of which the designer wants a full view; as shown in Figs. 1, 7-2 and 7-3, this point on the 275-ft-high building in the rear is marked X.

3. Determine the location of the picture plane and draw here the line L_p parallel to the secants spanning from S_L to S_R. Measure in the scale of the site plan at L_p the distance from S_L to S_R, here $P_{max} = 90$ ft. Also measure the distance $d_H = 400$ ft at a right angle between X and L_p.

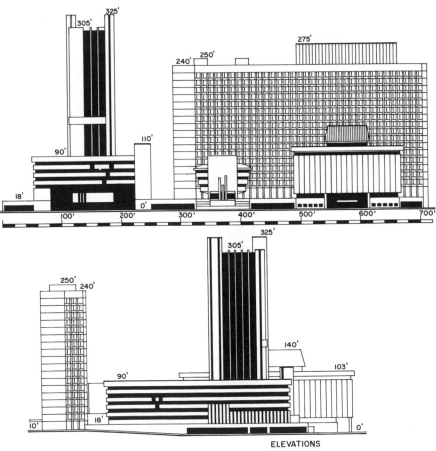

ELEVATIONS

Fig. 1, 7-2

4. To ascertain that the height of the object $H_o = 275$ ft plus a slight margin $m = 6$ ft, totaling 281 ft, is covered by the height of the perspective, the following equation has to be applied:

$$P_{o,\max} = \tfrac{4}{3}(H_o + m - \tfrac{1}{2}d_H)$$
$$= \tfrac{4}{3}(275' + 6' - \tfrac{1}{2} \times 400') = 108'$$

Extend the distance between S_L and S_R at LP from 90 ft to 108 ft and draw here a parallel to S_L.

Note: An increase of $P_{o,\max}$ obviously results in a wider and higher view. As long as a slight correction is necessary, as shown in Fig. 1, 7-3, the anticipated picture will not be affected by a broader illustration of the object. If, however, a considerable enlargement which could subdue the appearance of the main object becomes necessary, a moderate trespass of the circle of undistorted projection may be acceptable, unless the central perspective (Method 1, Chap. 1) is suitable.

5. Draw through the intersection of LP and S_R the line A parallel to the dash-point-dash calibration until it intersects S_L; then draw the line B to intersect the front line of the building in the rear.

Draw a second B line through the intersection of A and S_L in order to outline the rectangle AB. Measure A and B in any scale, thus obtaining the ratio $A:B$; in this case $A:B = 145':450' \approx 0.322'$.

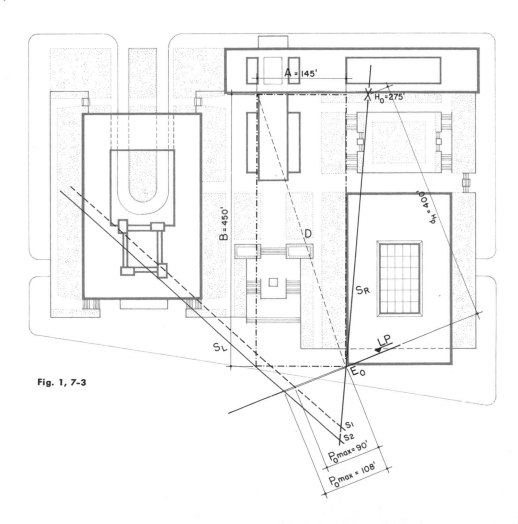

Fig. 1, 7-3

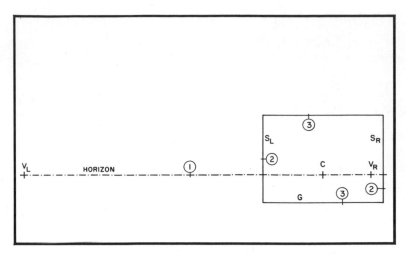

Fig. 1, 7-4

P_{max}: the Maximal Size of the Perspective

1. Draw the horizon on the lower part of the drawing board at a convenient height and locate the left vanishing point V_L and the right sideline S_R of the perspective.

   Note: If the rectangle AB is tilted to the right side (as seen in Fig. 1, 7-3), then the right sideline S_R and the left vanishing point V_L must be located. If the rectangle is tilted to the left, then the left sideline S_L and the right vanishing point must limit the horizon. The distance between V_L and S_R is T. In this demonstration $T = 60$ in.

2. P_{max} equals $\frac{1}{3}T$; in this case $\frac{1}{3} \times 60$ in. $= 20$ in. Scale off 20 in. from S_R to the left in order to locate S_L, the left side of P_{max}. Erect verticals at S_L and S_R.

3. The maximum height of the horizon was chosen for the purpose of this demonstration:

$$H_{H\ \mathrm{max}} = \frac{1}{4}P_{\mathrm{max}} = \frac{1}{4} \times 20'' = 5''$$

Scale off 5 in. from the horizon downward to determine the groundline G. The upper border of the perspective is $\frac{1}{2}P_{\mathrm{max}}$ above the horizon:

$$\frac{1}{2}P_{\mathrm{max}} = \frac{1}{2} \times 20'' = 10''$$

The location of the right vanishing point V_R is always set at 0.4 P_{max}, to be scaled off from C to the right, i.e.,

$$CV_R = 0.4\ P_{\mathrm{max}} = 0.4 \times 20'' = 8''$$

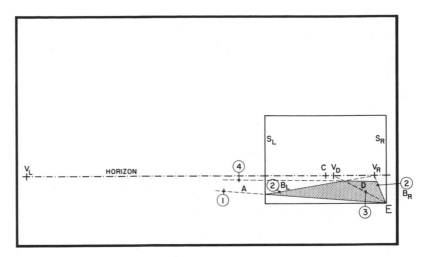

Fig. 1, 7-5

Determination of the Location of Point *E*

In this method the point *E*, where the rectangle *AB* touches the picture plane, coincides with the intersection of *G* at S_L if the rectangle is tilted to the left and with S_R when *AB* is tilted to the right, as shown in Fig. 1, 7-3.

1. Draw the perspective line *A* from *E* to the left vanishing point V_L until it intersects S_L.
2. Draw the two perspective lines B_L and B_R from the intersection of *A* at S_L and *E* to the right vanishing point V_R.
3. Draw the diagonal *D* pointing from *E* toward the rear to locate the rear side *A*. The following formula locates the vanishing point V_D of this diagonal:

$$V_L V_D = \frac{2.5}{A/B + 2.5} \quad V_L V_R = \frac{2.5}{0.322 + 2.5}\, 58'' = 51.4''$$

   Scale off $V_L V_D$ from V_L to the right; draw the diagonal from *E* to V_D until it intersects the side B_L.
4. Draw the perspective line from V_L through the intersection of *D* at B_L until intersecting B_R. This concludes the perspective outline of *AB*.

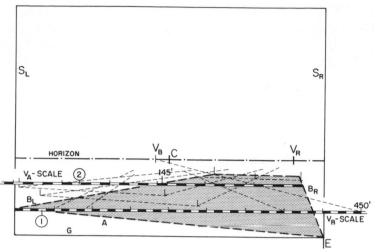

Fig. 1, 7-6

Completion of the Perspective, Part 1

1. Draw a measure line from the left corner of AB to S_L to the right, parallel to the horizon, as long as the drawing board permits. To determine the length of this measure line, select a scale which sets its length at 450 ft, which is the length of side B; then draw from the 450-ft mark a line through the left corner of AB in the rear until intersecting the horizon, thus locating the vanishing point V_B. All dimensions from ground-line to groundline parallel to A can now be scaled off on this measure line, called the V_B scale. They can be projected from the measure line perspectively upon B_L by perspective lines to V_B (see Fig. 1, 7-8). Project these marks on B_L upon AB by perspective lines from V_L into their correct depth.

2. To determine the length of these perspective lines according to the site plan, a second measure line has to be induced which determines the location of the corners of the object. Draw a second measure line from B_R to the left at any depth, not too distant from the V_B scale, parallel to the horizon. Select a scale of which the 145-ft mark, the length of side A, fits exactly between B_R and B_L and extend it to about 320 ft. This is the location on the site plan where S_L of the P.C. sheet cuts through the high tower on the left side, as shown in Fig. 1, 7-3.

   All dimensions from groundline to groundline parallel to B have to be scaled off on this measure line, the V_A scale. From here they are projected perspectively upon the respective perspective line converging at V_L by connection with V_R. V_R in this method is the appropriate vanishing point of the V_A scale. Erect verticals at those intersections where corners of the object appear (see perspective Fig. 1, 7-8).

This procedure requires the designer's attention and patience so that he can keep track of the crisscross line work which becomes necessary in finding the respective corners of the object.

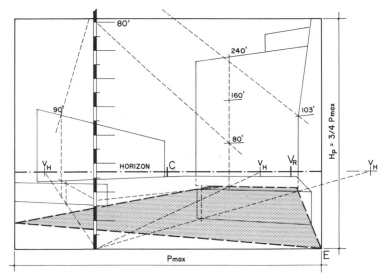

Fig. 1, 7-7

Completion of the Perspective, Part 2

The scale of this perspective has been determined by the PREPARATION OF THE SITE PLAN, step 4, page 76. The distance between S_L and S_R at L_P was extended from 90 ft to 180 ft; thus $S_L S_R = 108$ ft $= P_{o,\max}$.

In this demonstration the width of the perspective is $P_{\max} = SC = 20$ in.; consequently 20 in. represents the equivalent of 108 ft.

The height of the perspective, if correctly derived, is

$$\tfrac{3}{4} P_{\max} = \tfrac{3}{4} \times 20'' = 15'' \qquad \text{or} \qquad \tfrac{3}{4} \times 108' = 81'$$

i.e., 15 in. is the equivalent of 81 ft in height.

1. Erect a vertical measure line at a convenient location on the perspective from where one, two, or three perspective groundlines intersect as many as possible of the perspective lines to V_L and V_R. Divide the height into 81, 8.1, or 16.2 units, whichever is appropriate. Draw as many perspective groundlines as necessary to the horizon.
2. The intersection of such a groundline with the horizon marks the location of the respective vanishing point for all heights.
3. Erect a vertical where such a groundline intersects one of the perspective lines converging at V_L or V_R. Project the respective height from the vertical measure line upon the vertical by drawing a perspective line to the pertaining vanishing point (see perspective Fig. 1, 7-9).
4. Perspective lines to V_L and V_R from these projected heights complete the perspective.

Note: The high-rising building in the rear shown in Fig. 1, 7-9 was not immediately projected in its full height, because the vertical measure line proved to be too short. Therefore the height was subdivided into 3×80 ft $+ 35$ ft, as seen in Fig. 1, 7-7.

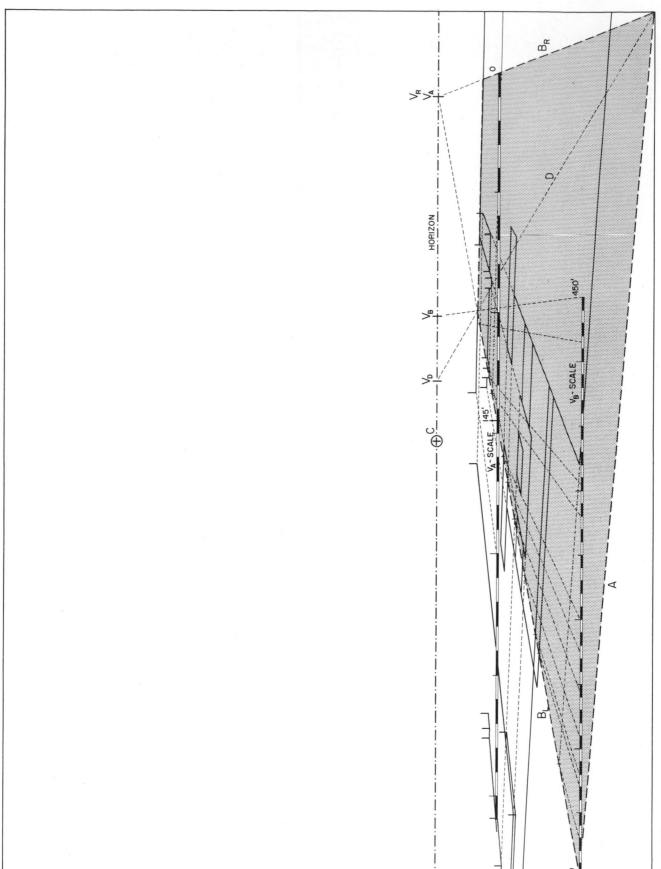

Fig. 1, 7-8

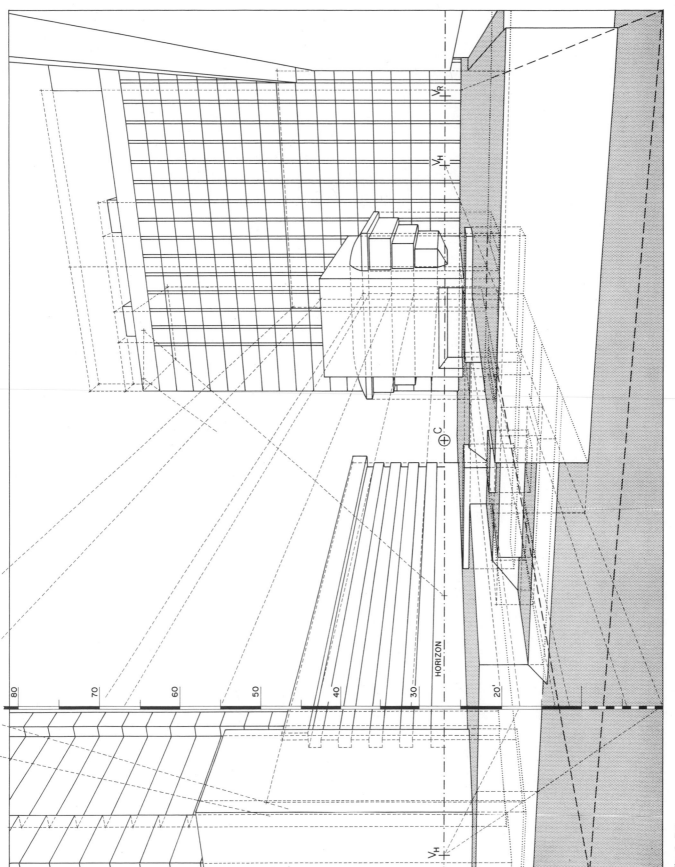

Fig. 1, 7-9

chapter two

BIRD'S-EYE PERSPECTIVES

INTRODUCTION

In the bird's-eye perspective the designer illustrates a view similar to the one seen by a flying bird. The impression he obtains from this viewpoint differs entirely from what he sees in a perspective at common eye level, which reflects a pedestrian view. A pedestrian standing among the objects on a plaza or street sees the buildings, trees, and walls related to each other in height and length. Perhaps several perspectives are necessary in order to obtain full information about the architectural characteristics of that specific building center.

The bird's-eye perspective illustrates the whole area at once. The heights of the objects are less important than the size of areas in their functional relationship, including sidewalks, roads, and greenery. It is a perspectively elaborated site plan. The architecture is evaluated as bas-relief rather than as a piece of sculpture.

What has been said before in the introduction to "Perspectives with Common Eye Level" stands also for the bird's-eye perspective, with the exception of the height of the horizon. It has been pointed out, in reference to the circle of undistorted projection, that men are more attentive to happenings below eye level. In a bird's-eye perspective it is even more important to properly determine the height of the horizon, because the whole object or building center will be below the horizon. It has been emphasized that, due to the limits of the circle of undistorted projection, the height of the horizon should never be larger than $\frac{1}{4}SC$ or one-fourth of the distance from the station point to the center of the picture (see Fig. 1, 0-3). Therefore this rule has to be adjusted to a bird's-eye perspective in order to reduce the areas beyond the circle of undistorted projection.

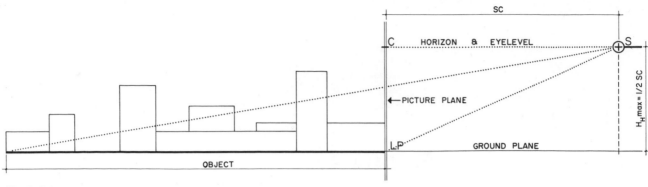

Fig. 2, 0-1

There are two types of bird's-eye perspectives. The first one is the less complicated and simulates a flight at a relatively low altitude. The pilot's eye, i.e., the observer's station point, looks straight ahead over the nose of the airplane. In other words, the line of sight is almost parallel to the ground plane, and the object to be pictured is visible on the ground in the circle of undistorted sight. The picture plane stands vertically upon the ground plane.

Figure 2, 0-1 shows this condition in a side elevation. Although unrealistic, it is geometrically correct. The projection of the object AB appears below the horizon on the lowest part of the picture plane. The height of the horizon is $\frac{1}{2}SC$. This is the maximum height which can be applied to this type of bird's-eye perspective.

Figure 2, 0-2 illustrates how the perspective of the object AB is confined to the circle of undistorted projection. If Fig. 1, 0-3 is compared to Fig. 2, 0-2, the difference in the size of the picture becomes obvious. The width has been changed from SC to $\frac{2}{3}SC$ and the height from $\frac{1}{4}SC$ to $\frac{1}{2}SC$; i.e., the elimination of the distortion in the bird's-eye perspective is achieved because of the size of the rendering. Using the same distance from the picture plane and the same position of the object AB, the perspective at common eye level ($\frac{1}{4}SC$) will always be larger than that of the bird's-eye perspective with an eye level equal to $\frac{1}{2}SC$.

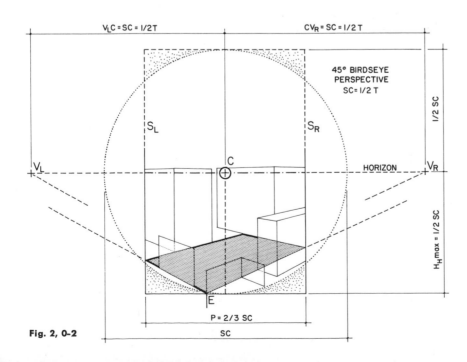

Fig. 2, 0-2

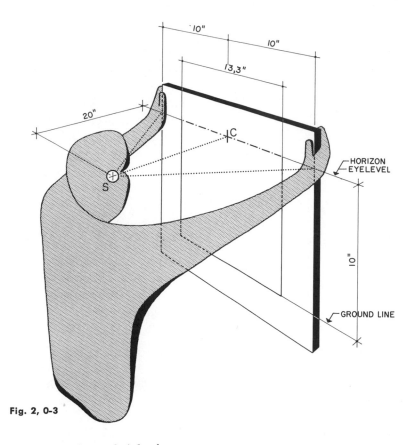

Fig. 2, 0-3

The designer has to adhere to the recommended maximum height, because the diameter of the circle of undistorted projection is equal to *SC* and will remain unchanged in all methods of this book.

The main characteristic of this type of bird's-eye perspective is that all vertical lines, edges, and corners of the object are also vertical in perspective, respectively parallel to each other. This simplifies the process of drawing.

Figure 2, 0-3 is equivalent to Fig. 1, 0-1. The difference between them, however, is obvious. In Fig. 2, 0-3 the perspective is below eye level, which, in this case, constitutes the upper border of the picture. This position is correct. The observer looks down upon the object as presumed. This is a position to which the observer of a picture is unaccustomed, especially if the rendering is on display in a row with perspectives of common eye level. The

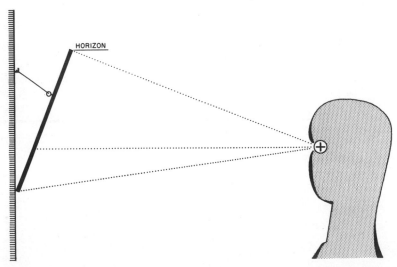

Fig. 2, 0-4

same effect can be achieved by slightly raising and tilting the picture. (See Fig. 2, 0-4 and compare to Fig. 2, 0-3.) Figure 2, 0-4 shows in side elevation the tilted picture on the wall, where the observer views it under approximately the same conditions as those under which the perspective was done; thus distortion is avoided. The procedure of raising and tilting also has the advantage that the rendering can be aligned in height with other perspectives on display. The tilt angle is a matter of judgment; no strict rules can be presented for this case.

The second type of bird's-eye perspective simulates the situation of a descending airplane, from which the pilot looks straight ahead over the nose of the plane into the center of an area. Figure 2, 0-5 illustrates the situation unrealistically, while the geometrical conditions have been set into correct correlation. Although the same object is kept in the same distance from station point S as shown in Fig. 2, 0-1, four differences become obvious.

1. The picture plane is tilted, yet remains at right angles with the central line of sight SC.

2. Center C no longer coincides with the line of the horizon; i.e., the plane of horizon and the plane of eye level are two separated planes which intersect in the line through the station point S parallel to the picture plane and horizontal to the ground plane.

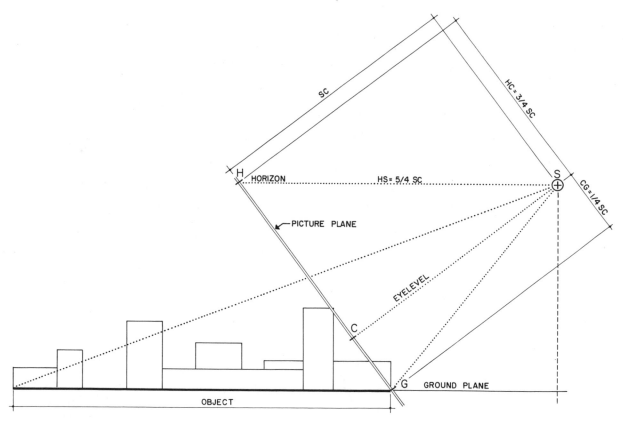

Fig. 2, 0-5

3. The height of the perspective is greater than that of the perspective in Fig. 2, 0-1.

4. A third vanishing point V_C appears plumb below the center C of the perspective (see Fig. 2, 2-1b).

A perspective may have as many vanishing points as an object has planes, lines, and edges *nonparallel* to the picture plane. For the purpose of simplification it is assumed that in this instance the object is the rectangle AB with two parallel sides pointing to the right vanishing point V_R, two parallel sides pointing to the left vanishing point V_L, and the upright planes which enclose the rectangle pointing to the third vanishing point V_C. In contrast to all other perspectives the vertical lines of the object do not appear as vertical parallels, but converge into the third vanishing point, thereby creating the optical illusion of looking into the ravines of skyscrapers (see Fig. 2, 0-6).

It is not advisable to make excessive use of the third vanishing point. It easily brings irrelevant details such as roofs and chimneys to the foreground and magnifies them. They are relatively unimportant to the entire building complex and to the layout. The difficulty in drawing a bird's-eye perspective with the third vanishing point lies in the art of describing in a realistic manner what in fact is occurring. The purpose of a perspective is still to present a true illustration of an architectural project.

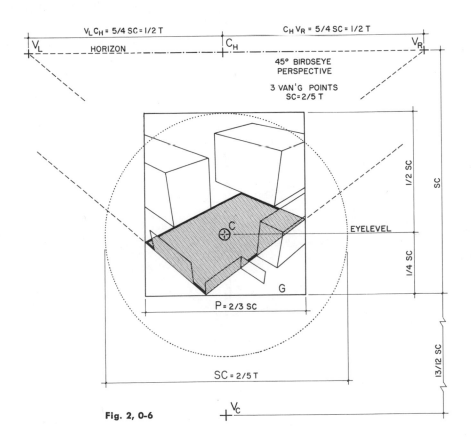

Fig. 2, 0-6

METHOD 1: Bird's-eye Perspective with Two Vanishing Points

Characteristics

The construction of this perspective is based upon the preceding methods in Chap. 1 for the construction of perspectives with common eye level.

The designer chooses one of the previously described methods in order to determine the center and the vanishing points of the planned bird's-eye perspective. Hence, the characteristics of the bird's-eye perspective will change according to the specifically selected case. However, all the methods to be employed here have certain features in common:

1. P_{max} is usually $\frac{2}{3}SC$; it is never greater, although sometimes smaller.
2. The height of the horizon H_H equals at least $\frac{1}{2}SC$ and cannot be less than $\frac{3}{4}P_{max}$. If this is not satisfactory and the horizon cannot be raised because of a limited drawing board, then P_{max} must be reduced.
3. The plan of the object, the site plan, will be immediately projected into the desired perspective by using the focus of projection F_p which eliminates the V_A and V_B scales.
4. The detailed preparation of the site plan is eliminated; only the rectangle AB remains. A P_H projection is not necessary.

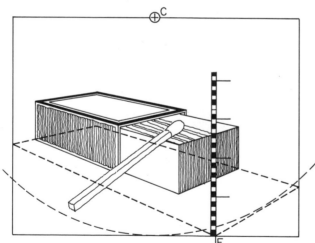

Fig. 2, 1-1

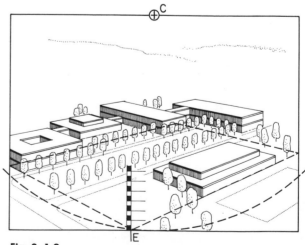

Fig. 2, 1-2

Applicability

This type of perspective is the all-round perspective. Whether a matchbox, a campus plan, an object twice as high as the eye level, or the interior of a cathedral must be illustrated, this method, properly applied, offers a unique variety of possibilities (see Figs. 2, 1-1– 1-4).

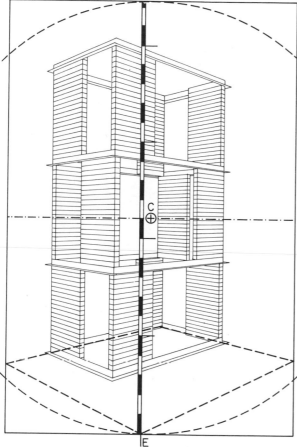

Fig. 2, 1-3

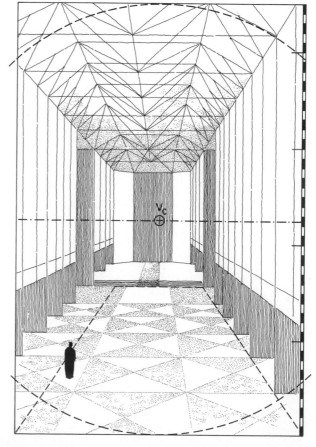

Fig. 2, 1-4

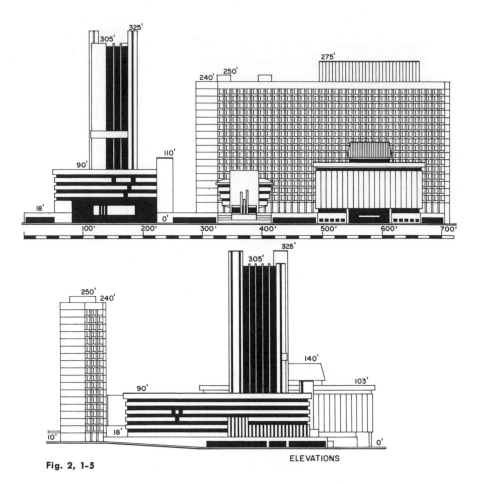

Fig. 2, 1-5

ELEVATIONS

The Rectangle AB

Enclose that part of the object to be illustrated by drawing the rectangle AB and measure its sides A and B in any scale in order to obtain the ratio $A:B$, provided that A and B are measured in the same scale. In this demonstration the ratio is $A:B = 400':560' = 5:7 = 0.71$ (see Fig. 2, 1-6).

P_{max}: the Maximal Size of the Perspective

Choose one of the previously described methods of Chap. 1 and derive SC by the specific formula of that case in order to locate C, the center of the perspective. Method 4, the 45° perspective, was selected for the following demonstration (see Fig. 1, 4-1).

1. Draw the horizon on the upper part of the drawing board so that the focus of the projection F_p at the distance of SC plumb below C is still on the drawing board; then locate the vanishing points V_L and V_R.

2. Bisect the distance T between V_L and V_R, in this demonstration $T = 60$ in., mark it C, and drop a perpendicular. Scale off $SC = \frac{1}{2}T = \frac{1}{2} \times 60$ in. = 30 in. from C downward and mark it F_p.

3. $P_{max} = \frac{2}{3}SC = \frac{1}{3}T = \frac{1}{3} \times 60$ in. = 20 in. Lay off 10 in. to the left and right of C, locating S_L and S_R. Drop perpendiculars as the left and right sidelines of the perspective.

4. The height H_p of the perspective is $\frac{1}{2}SC = \frac{1}{2} \times 30$ in. = 15 in. Scale off 15 in. from the horizon downward and draw the groundline G, connecting S_L and S_R.

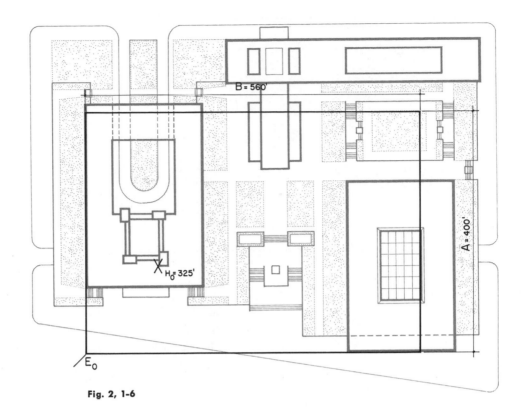

B = 560'

A = 400'

$H_o = 325'$

E_o

Fig. 2, 1-6

T

V_L C   HORIZON V_R

①

S_L S_R

③   ②   ③   1/2 SC

G

④   SC

1/2 Pmax= 1/3 SC   1/2 Pmax

45°- PERSPECTIVE

F_P

SC = 1/2 T   SC

Fig. 2, 1-7

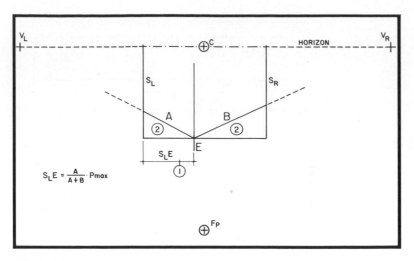

Fig. 2, 1-8

Determination of the Location of Point E

1. To construct the perspective in accordance with the perspective of the rectangle AB and its position to the picture plane, it is essential to locate properly E, the point at which the nearest corner of AB touches the picture plane.

   The respective formula for $S_L E$ in the 45° perspective is

   $$S_L E = \frac{A}{A + B} P_{\max} = \frac{400'}{400' + 560'} 20'' = 8.35''$$

   Scale off $S_L E = 8.35$ in. from S_L to the right, locating E, and erect the vertical in E.

2. To locate sides A and B, draw perspective lines from E to V_L and V_R until they intersect S_L and S_R.

Final Adjustment of the Width of the Perspective

Since the size of the perspective is determined either by the size of the drawing board or by the designer's choice, there is no relationship between the scale of the object and that of the perspective. To establish the proportionate height of the object in this picture, it is essential to know its scale. Use one of the three solutions in Chap. 3, Method 4, in order to convert a perspective line into the true length of the respective scale.

In the following demonstration Method 4, Solution c has been applied:

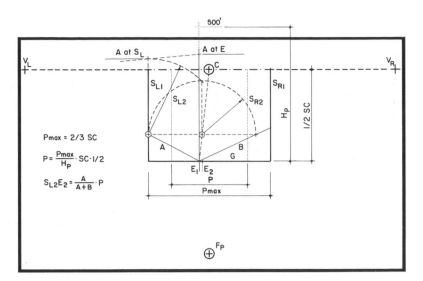

Fig. 2, 1-9

1. Draw the horizontal from S_L at the intersection of EV_L to the right, intersecting EV_R. Connect E with C, bisecting the horizontal. Erect the vertical at the bisection to locate the zenith of the semicircle and rotate the zenith from the intersection of A at S_L in order to locate the perspectively reduced side A upon S_L; project side A upon the vertical at E by drawing a perspective line from V_L through A at S_L; and continue until intersecting the vertical at E. The length of side A in this example is 400 ft (see Fig. 2, 1-6). Its equivalent for this perspective is the distance between A and G at E.

2. See perspective Fig. 2, 1-12. The A at E or 400-ft mark is above the horizon. The calibration of the vertical at E into 40 units, each 10 ft, shows that the 325-ft-high tower of the demonstrated object is below the horizon.

This is satisfactory for the purpose of this perspective. Therefore, the values of the height of the horizon and the width of the perspective remain as previously established. However, a 450-ft-high tower poses a problem if the designer does not accept an illustration of the object as shown in Fig. 2, 1-3, but prefers an horizon fairly above the highest point of the object.

Because of the limited size of the drawing board, 60 in., the horizon cannot be raised without distorting the layout of AB on the ground plane, and P_{max} must be reduced to P.

In a case like this, the designer has to scale off the required height, in this example 450 ft, plus a certain margin 50 ft at E; then measure to the same scale the width of the perspective in order to obtain the ratio $P_{max}:H_p$, here $455':500' \approx 0.91$ (see Fig. 2, 1-9).

The formula

$$P = \frac{P_{max}}{H_p} \frac{1}{2} SC = 0.91 \times \frac{1}{2} \times 30'' = 13.6''$$

answers the question for the reduction of P_{max} to P.

Note: Any change of the perspective's width requires the relocation of point E to E_2 (see Fig. 2, 1-9) by employing the respective $S_L E$ formula, in this case

$$S_{L2}E_2 = \frac{A}{A+B} P$$

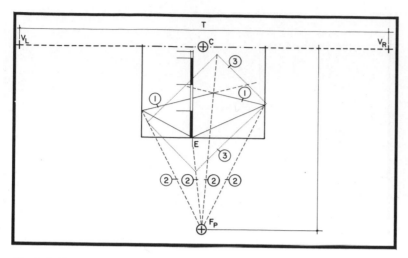

Fig. 2, 1-10

Placement of the Site Plan under the Perspective

In order to project the site plan immediately into perspective, its position must be properly related to A, B, E, and F_p for locating each point of the site plan in its correct perspective position.

It eases the projection if the diagonal AB in the site plan is approximately as long as the width of the perspective.

1. Draw perspective lines from the intersection of A at S_L to V_R and from the intersection of B at S_R to V_L in order to locate the fourth corner of AB in the rear.

2. Connect all four corners of AB with F_p, forming a four-sided pyramid upside down.

3. Place the site plan under the perspective transparency at an angle of 45° in such a way that all four corners of AB in the site plan fall in line with the four edges of the pyramid (see perspective Fig. 2, 1-12).

Note: The angle under which the site plan has to be placed must be the same at which the site plan is positioned to the picture plane. AB is therefore turned to 45°, because the 45° bird's-eye perspective is being demonstrated. If point E is carefully located, then the four corners of AB will be exactly on the edges of the pyramid.

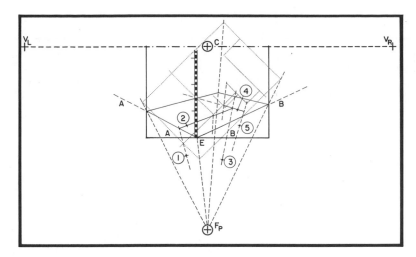

Fig. 2, 1-11

Completion of the Perspective

1. Choose one characteristic line in the site plan intersecting A and project the point of intersection upon A, the side A in perspective, by connecting it with F_p. (See also perspective Fig. 2, 1-12.)

2. Draw a perspective line from the projected point to the vanishing point V_R.

3. Project the end of this line in the site plan upon the perspective line by connection to F_p.

4. Draw the perspective line from this projected point to the vanishing point V_L.

5. Again project the end of this line in the site plan upon the last perspective line by connection to F_p and continue from point to point until the necessary corners of the object have been projected into the perspective plan. Erect verticals at every point and transfer the respective height from the calibrated vertical at E to each corner according to Chap. 3, Method 5. Complete the perspective by drawing perspective lines from the elevation marks to the respective vanishing points.

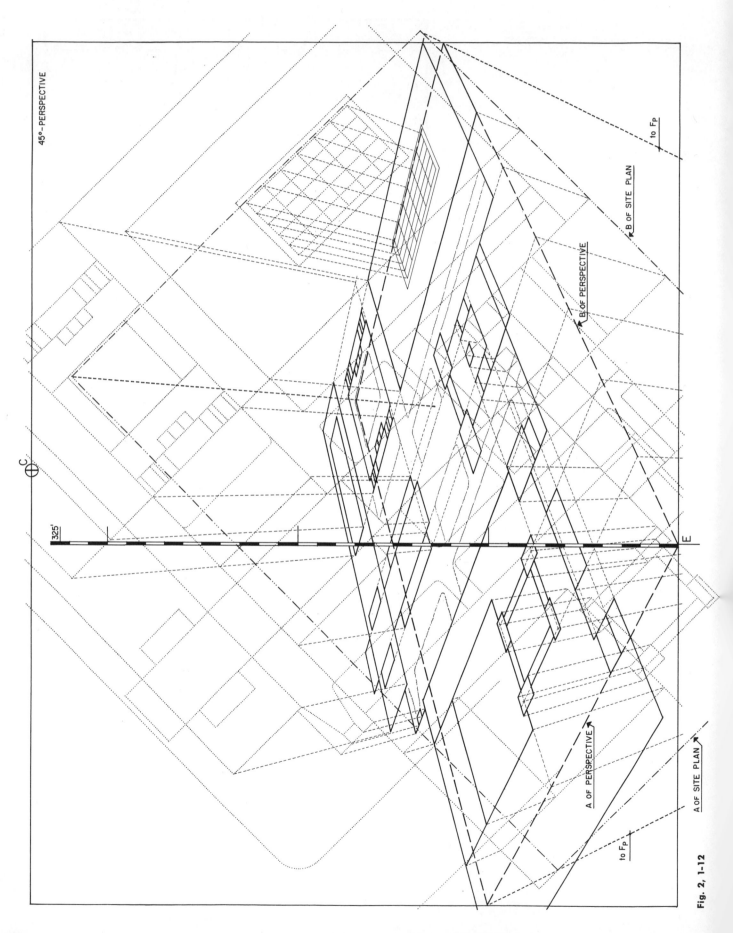

45°- PERSPECTIVE

B OF SITE PLAN

B OF PERSPECTIVE

to Fp

A OF PERSPECTIVE

A OF SITE PLAN

to Fp

325'

E

Fig. 2, 1-12

98

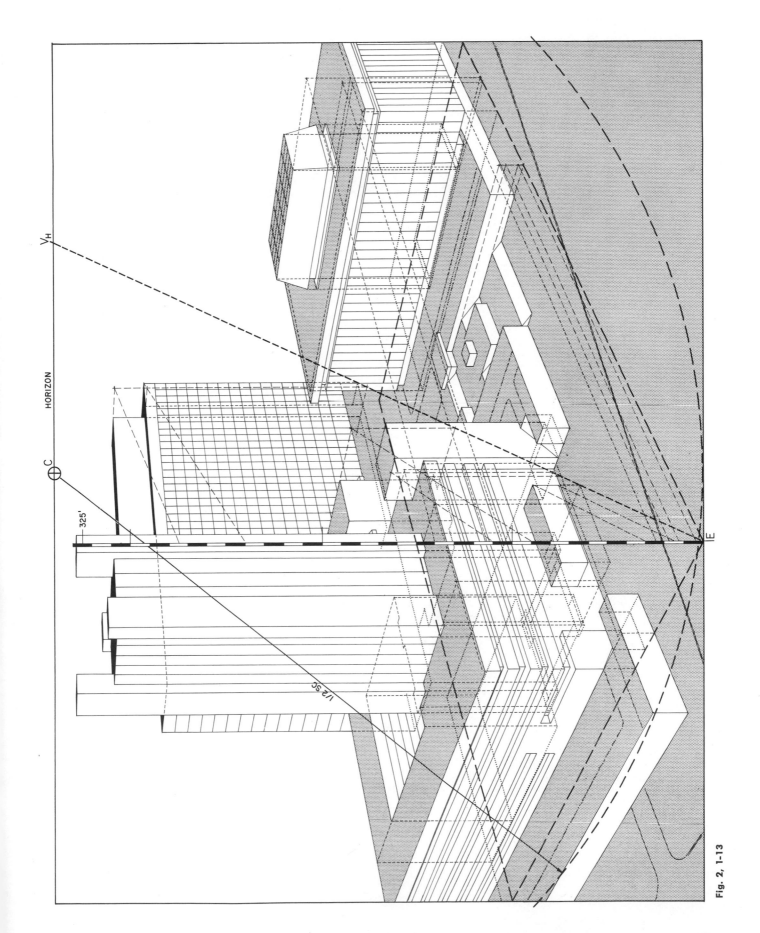

HORIZON

C

V_H

325'

1/2 SC

E

Fig. 2, 1-13

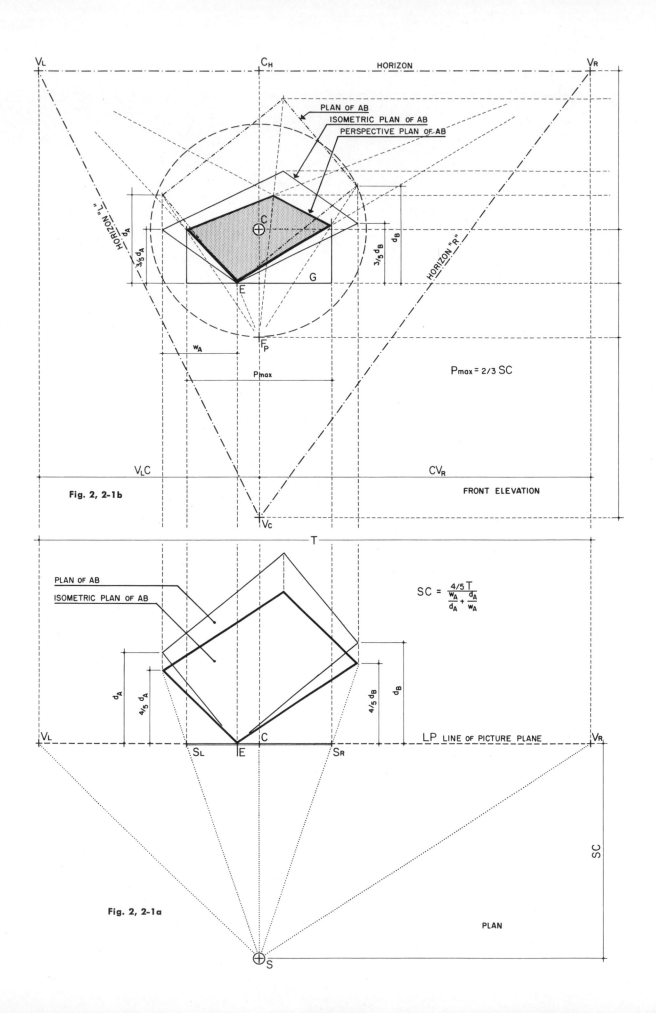

HORIZON

C_H

V_L V_R

PLAN OF AB

ISOMETRIC PLAN OF AB

PERSPECTIVE PLAN OF AB

HORIZON "L"

d_A

$3/5\,d_A$

C

d_B

$3/5\,d_B$

HORIZON "R"

G

E

F_P

w_A

P_{max}

$P_{max} = 2/3\ SC$

V_LC CV_R

Fig. 2, 2-1b   FRONT ELEVATION

V_C

T

PLAN OF AB

ISOMETRIC PLAN OF AB

$$SC = \frac{4/5\ T}{\dfrac{w_A}{d_A} + \dfrac{d_A}{w_A}}$$

d_A

$4/5\,d_A$

d_B

$4/5\,d_B$

V_L LP LINE OF PICTURE PLANE V_R

S_L E   C S_R

SC

Fig. 2, 2-1a

PLAN

S

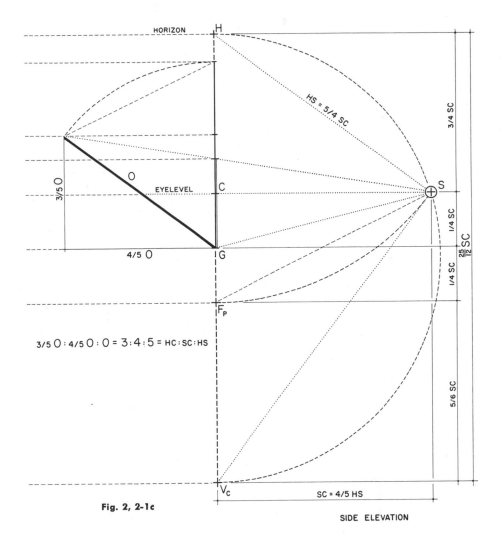

Fig. 2, 2-1c

$3/5\,O : 4/5\,O : O = 3:4:5 = HC:SC:HS$

SIDE ELEVATION

METHOD 2: Bird's-eye Perspective with Three Vanishing Points

Characteristics

The ground plane on which the object rests is, in geometric terms, tilted toward the picture plane forming a right triangle with the ratio 3:4:5 of its three sides (see Fig. 2, 2-1c, showing $\frac{3}{5} \times 0$ and $\frac{4}{5} \times 0$ as small sides of the triangle and 0 as hypotenuse and base of the object AB). This ratio determines the height of the horizon, the location of the center C of the perspective below the horizon, and the depth of the third vanishing point V_C below the horizon, depending on the length of SC (see Fig. 2, 2-1c). The inclination of the ground plane affects the shape of the rectangle AB in plan, which changes to the parallelogram AB (see Fig. 2, 2-1a). The location of the vanishing points is determined by $\frac{5}{4}SC$, which is the length of the line of sight HS parallel to the ground plane (see Fig. 2, 2-1c). This in turn affects the formula for SC:

$$HS = \tfrac{5}{4}SC = \frac{T}{w_A/d_A + d_A/w_A}$$

$$SC = \frac{\tfrac{4}{5}T}{w_A/d_A + d_A/w_A}$$

101

Consequently

$$V_L C_H = \frac{w_A}{d_A} \times \frac{5}{4} SC$$

$$C_H V_R = \frac{d_A}{w_A} \times \frac{5}{4} SC$$

1. P_{max} is usually $\frac{2}{3}SC$.
2. The height of the horizon is SC, measured from the groundline G.
3. The center C of the perspective is $\frac{1}{4}SC$ above G.
4. The focus of projection F_p from which the plan of the object is immediately projected into perspective is $\frac{1}{4}SC$ below G.
5. The third vanishing point V_C is $1\frac{3}{12}SC$ below G.

These listed data are fixed. As T varies so does SC, but the coefficient of SC is constant.

Applicability

The successful use of this method is limited by the requirement that the center line of the perspective should be near the midpoint between V_L and V_R. This excludes Method 5, the 30°/60° perspective, and Method 7, the use of the transparent sheet, in Chap. 1. All other methods can be employed as long as either side A or side B of the rectangle in Methods 1 and 3 or the angles α and β of the rectangle's position in Methods 4 and 6 do not differ too much from each other. Method 1, the central perspective, has no limitation.

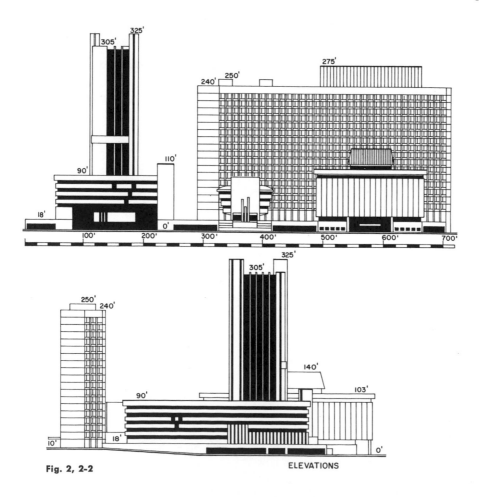

Fig. 2, 2-2   ELEVATIONS

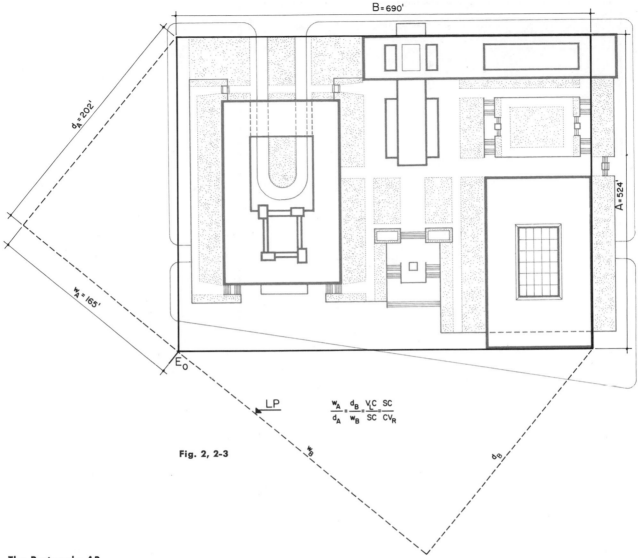

$$\frac{w_A}{d_A} = \frac{d_B}{w_B} = \frac{V_C}{SC} = \frac{SC}{CV_R}$$

Fig. 2, 2-3

The Rectangle AB

Enclose that part of the object to be illustrated by drawing the rectangle *AB* (see concluding note on the height of the object, page 108). Scale off its sides *A* and *B* in any scale in order to obtain the ratio *A*:*B*, provided that *A* and *B* are measured in the same scale. In this demonstration the ratio is $A:B = 524':690' = 0.76$ (see Fig. 2, 2-3).

$P_{\max}$: the Maximal Size of the Perspective and Determination of the Third Vanishing Point V_C

For the following demonstration Method 6, Chap. 1, was chosen, in which the designer determines the angles of position α and β (see Fig. 1, 6-1). This method requires more details from the site plan in order to obtain the ratio $d_A:w_A$, which locates the left and right vanishing points V_L and V_R.

1. Draw through the foremost corner E_o on the site plan the straight line *LP* to establish the angle of position at which the object is to be seen.

2. Drop the perpendiculars d_A and w_A from the left and right corners of *AB* upon *LP*. Scale off in any scale d_A and w_A. In this demonstration the ratio is $d_A:w_A = 202':165' = 1.22$, and $w_A:d_A = 165':202' = 0.82$ (see Fig. 2, 2-3).

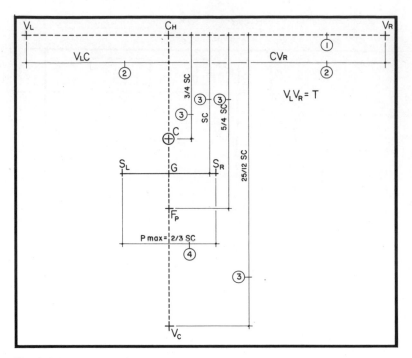

Fig. 2, 2-4

With these data the location of the center C and the maximal size P_{max} can be derived.

1. Draw the horizon as high as possible on the drawing board. A square-shaped drawing board should be used, as shown in Fig. 2, 2-4. Locate V_L and V_R. In this demonstration the distance T between V_L and V_R measures 52.5 in.

2. Determine SC, the main sight line from the station point S to the center C of the perspective, by the formula

$$SC = \frac{0.8T}{w_A/d_A + d_A/w_A} = \frac{0.8 \times 52.5''}{0.82 + 1.22} = \frac{42''}{2.04} = 20.6''$$

in order to locate the center line of the perspective on the horizon by the formulas

$$V_L C = \frac{w_A}{d_A} \times \frac{5}{4} SC = 0.82 \times 1.25 \times 20.6'' = 21.0''$$

$$CV_R = \frac{d_A}{w_A} \times \frac{5}{4} SC = 1.22 \times 1.25 \times 20.6'' = \underline{31.5''}$$
$$\underline{52.5''} = T$$

Scale off $V_L C$ from V_L to the right, mark the point C_H, and drop a perpendicular.

3. Locate the following points on this perpendicular by scaling off the respective distance from C_H on downward:

Center of the perspective C

$$C_H C = \tfrac{3}{4} SC = 0.75 \times 20.6'' = 15.5''$$

Groundline G

$$C_H G = SC = 20.6''$$

Focus of projection F_p

$$C_H F_p = \tfrac{5}{4} SC = 1.25 \times 20.6'' = 25.8''$$

Third vanishing point V_C

$$C_H V_C = {}^{25}\!/_{12} SC = 2.08 \times 20.6'' = 43.0''$$

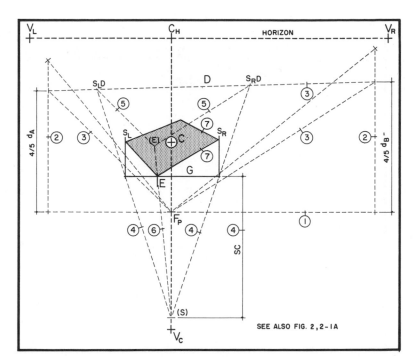

Fig. 2, 2-5

4. Compared to Method 6, Chap. 1, where $P_{max} = SC = 25.6$ in.,

$$P_{max} = \tfrac{2}{3}SC = 0.67 \times 20.6'' = 13.75''$$

the result here for P_{max}, 13.75 in., is small. This is characteristic of the bird's-eye perspective with three vanishing points. Increasing P_{max} by keeping $T = 52.5$ in. and $C_H V_C = 43$ in., the farther the vertical lines of the object are from the center line the more they diverge and appear unrealistic. For this reason, this appropriate method was chosen for the demonstration. It reduces P_{max} drastically and limits the divergence of the vertical sidelines without forcing the designer to use oversized drafting tools.

Determination of the Location of Point E (graphical)

1. Draw the horizontal through F_p all the way across the drawing board.
2. Connect F_p with V_L and V_R, scale off in any scale A on $V_L F_p$ and B on $F_p V_R$ from F_p upward, and drop the perpendiculars d_A and d_B.
3. Reduce d_A and d_B by one-fifth and connect the reduced perpendiculars with F_p and draw diagonal D.
4. Scale off SC from G downward to locate (S), connect (S) with $S_L G$ and $G S_R$, and continue in order to locate $S_L D$ and $S_R D$ on D.
5. Draw parallels to the line $F_p \tfrac{4}{5}d_A$ and to the line $F_p \tfrac{4}{5}d_B$ through $S_R D$ and $S_L D$ to locate the auxiliary point (E) at their intersection.
6. Connect (E) with (S) to locate E on G.
7. Draw perspective lines from E to V_L and V_R until intersecting S_L and S_R and complete the perspective layout of AB by drawing perspective lines from S_L and S_R to V_L and V_R.

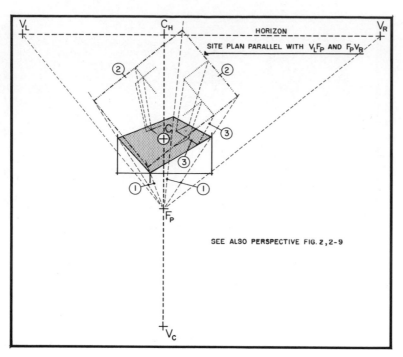

Fig. 2, 2-6

Placement of the Site Plan under the Perspective Layout of AB

1. Connect all four corners of the perspective layout AB with F_p.
2. Place the rectangle of the site plan under the transparent sheet of the perspective in such a way that the sides A and B are parallel with $V_L F_p$ and $F_p V_R$ and that all corners of AB touch the four corner lines of the perspective layout of AB converging at F_p.

   Note: If the location of point E has been properly determined according to instructions, then all four corners of the site plan align with the corner lines of the perspective layout, converging at F_p. If this test proves the accuracy of the location of the point E, then all other points of the site plan will fall exactly into their perspective place by connection with F_p.

3. Continue the perspective layout of AB by drawing one characteristic line which intersects one of the four boundary lines of the site plan. Project this point into perspective by connecting it with F_p. Draw a perspective line to the respective vanishing point and step from point to point until the front lines of the object are projected. Perspective Fig. 2, 2-9 illustrates this procedure. For clarity the whole plan of each part of the object has been laid out. In practice it is not necessary to do so.

The Scale of the Perspective, Part A

As described in Chap. 1, no immediate relationship exists between the scale of the perspective and that of the object. In these methods the derived scale was calibrated by equal units of either feet or inches. Notice that in this method the scale decreases as it comes closer to the third vanishing point V_C.

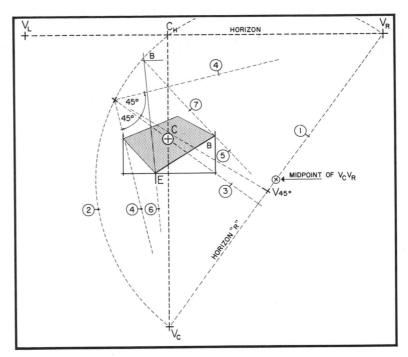

Fig. 2, 2-7

Note: Every line leading to a vanishing point shrinks in scale as demonstrated by the perspectively projected V_A and V_B scales shown in all perspective figures in Chap. 1.

Each side of AB can be used as a basic measurement for the vertical scale at E, which is vertical in reality but not in perspective.

1. Draw a second horizon by connecting V_C and V_R.
2. Rotate V_C or V_R from the midpoint of V_C and V_R to a semicircle.
3. Drop a perpendicular from C upon $V_C V_R$ and continue above C in order to intersect the semicircle.
4. Draw lines from this intersection at the semicircle to V_C and V_R. They form a right angle.
5. Bisect the right angle in order to locate V_{45} on the horizon $V_C V_R$.
6. Draw a perspective line from V_C through E and extend it beyond C.
7. Draw a perspective line from V_{45} through the right corner of AB in order to intersect the perspective line from V_C through E. This point marks the perspective length of B upon the perspective line $V_C E$. In Fig. 2, 2-8, it represents 690 ft, which is the length of B in the site plan (see Fig. 2, 2-3).

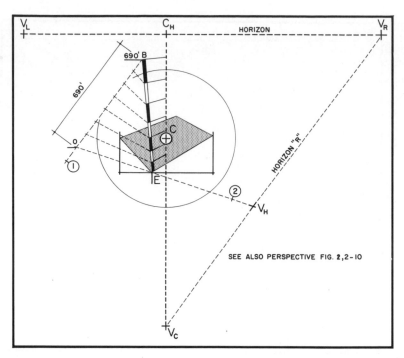

Fig. 2, 2-8

The Scale of the Perspective, Part B

1. Draw a parallel to $V_C V_R$ downward from the B mark on the line from V_C through E. Divide this line into equal units reflecting the scale of $B = 690$ ft.

2. Connect the last unit with E and continue beyond E in order to locate V_H on the $V_C V_R$ horizon. Project all units upon the perspective line $V_C E$ by drawing perspective lines from each unit to V_H. This calibrates perspectively the perspective line at E from which every height of the object can be projected into the perspective by the auxiliary Method 5 in Chap. 3 (see Fig. 2, 2-10).

Concluding Note on the Height of the Object: In Fig. 2, 2-8 the perspective scale, representing perspectively the length of side B, exceeds the circle of undistorted projection. Thus, a height of an object which is by far longer than one of the rectangle's sides A or B would considerably exceed the circle or could even reach over the horizon, producing obvious and undesirable enlargements in the upper part of the perspective. To prevent this, the one side of AB to be projected as the vertical scale upon $V_C E$ should be at least as long as the height of the object.

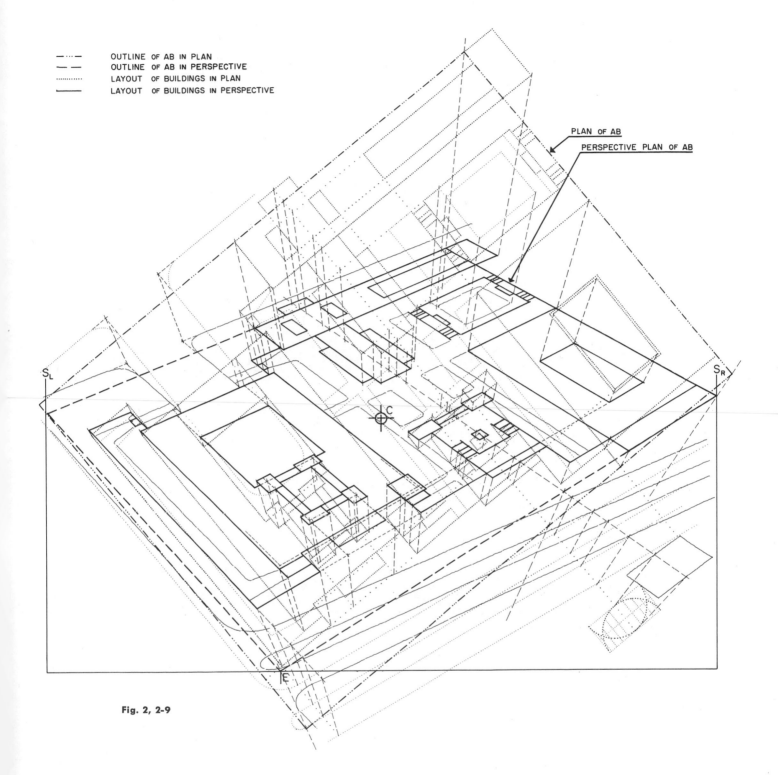

OUTLINE OF AB IN PLAN
OUTLINE OF AB IN PERSPECTIVE
LAYOUT OF BUILDINGS IN PLAN
LAYOUT OF BUILDINGS IN PERSPECTIVE

PLAN OF AB
PERSPECTIVE PLAN OF AB

S_L

S_R

C

E

Fig. 2, 2-9

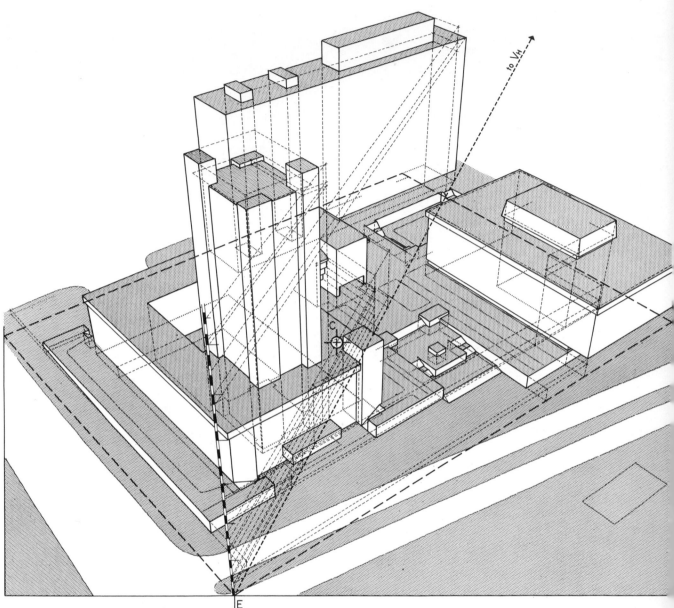

Fig. 2, 2-10

110

chapter three

AUXILIARY METHODS

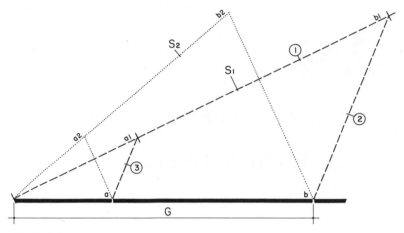

Fig. 3, 1-1

METHOD 1: Division of a Line at a Given Ratio

Problem

The groundline G has to be proportionally divided at a ratio $a:b$.

Solution

1. Draw the line S_1 at any suitable angle to G, beginning at one end of G (see Fig. 3, 1-1), and lay off the sections a and b in any convenient scale. The dotted-line construction shows the same procedure; yet line S_2 is drawn in a different scale. Both scales S_1 and S_2 divide G at the same ratio, because $a_1:b_1 = a_2:b_2$.
2. Connect b_1 with the end of G.
3. Draw a parallel to this line through a_1 in order to locate a on G. This completes the proportional division of G at a ratio $a:b$.

Note: The line G may be any line. It can be proportionally divided by any number of sections, as shown in Fig. 3, 1-2.

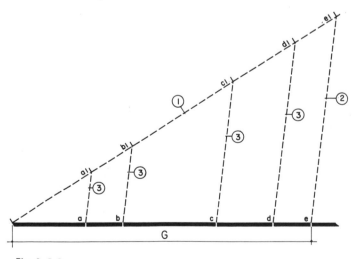

Fig. 3, 1-2

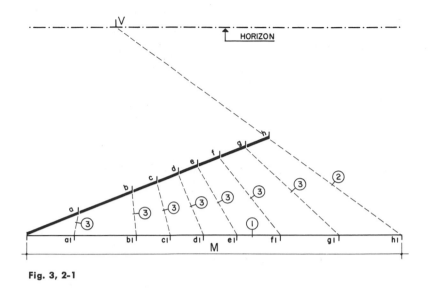

Fig. 3, 2-1

METHOD 2: Proportionate Division of a Line in Perspective

Problem

A certain number of consecutive sections has to be perspectively projected upon a specific straight line whose length is known.

Solution

1. Draw a measure line M parallel to the horizon beginning at the nearest end of the respective line in perspective, as shown in Fig. 3, 2-1. Measure from this end consecutively toward the right the sections a, b, c, and d, which are to be projected by using any suitable scale.
2. Connect the last section of the graduated line with the end of the line to be perspectively divided, continue until intersecting the horizon, and mark the intersection V.
3. Draw from each section of the calibrated line a connection to V, intersecting the line in perspective. Each intersection marks the projected section a, b, c, or d.

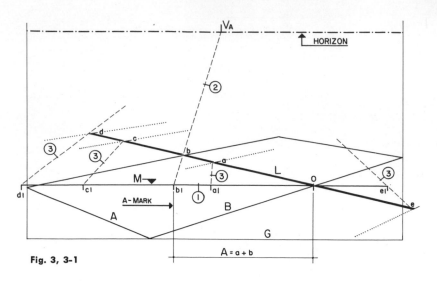

Fig. 3, 3-1

METHOD 3:   Division of a Perspective Line Overlapping the Rectangle *AB*

Problem

The perspective line *L* overlapping the rectangle *AB* has to be proportionally graduated by a given number of sections *a*, *b*, *c*, *d*, and *e*.

Solution

1. Draw a parallel to the groundline *G* through the intersection *O* of the nearest side *B* and line *L* to be divided (see Fig. 3, 3-1). Measure off the sections a_1 through d_1 to the left and e_1 to the right of point *O* in any scale.
2. Connect the *A* mark of line *M* with the intersection of *L* and *B* in the rear and continue until intersecting the horizon, thereby locating the vanishing point V_A for this projection.
3. Draw perspective lines from each section of the calibrated line to V_A in order to locate the projections upon *L*.

This demonstration shows how to divide perspectively a straight line parallel to the side *A* of the rectangle *AB*.

Figure 3, 3-2 shows the previously calibrated line and its perspective lines converging in the vanishing point V_R. In addition it illustrates the division of a line parallel to the side *B*. This process is similar to the preceding division in Fig. 3, 3-1, in that it locates the various points of the perspective.

Figures 3, 3-1 and 3-2 illustrate the relation of each point to sides *A* and *B* or to each one of their parallels whether the points are in the area of the rectangle *AB* or beyond it.

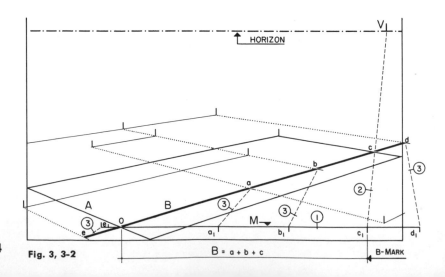

Fig. 3, 3-2

METHOD 4: Determination of the Object's Height by Derivation of the Perspective's Equivalent Scale

Since the size of the perspective has not been related to the scale of the object because the construction of the perspective had to fit the drawing board, the equivalent scale of the perspective has to be derived by setting the dimensions of the object in relation to those of the perspective. The three following solutions show how to determine the correct scale of a perspective.

Problem

Derive the equivalent scale of the perspective, thus determining the object's height in perspective.

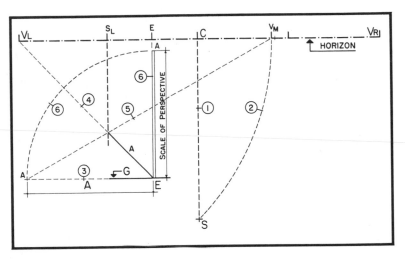

Fig. 3, 4–1

Method 4, Solution a: Measure-line Method

1. Drop a perpendicular from C and lay off SC to locate S. SC is calculated by the following formula:

$$SC = \sqrt{V_L C \times CV_R}$$

2. Rotate S from V_L upward, locating V_M on the horizon.
3. Draw, as low as possible, an auxiliary groundline G after determination of the location of E (see Chap. 3, Method 7).
4. Draw from E at G a perspective line to the nearest of the vanishing points until intersecting one of the sidelines. Figure 3, 4-1 shows the line from E to V_L intersecting S_L.
5. Draw from V_M a perspective line through the intersection of A and S_L, locating point A on G.
6. Rotate point A from E upward to locate A upon the vertical at E. The distance between point A and E at G is the true length of side A in this perspective. It is the scale for the various heights of the object.

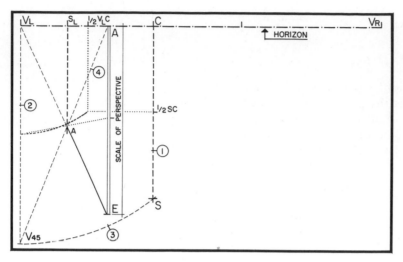

Fig. 3, 4-2

Method 4, Solution *b*: 45° Diagonal Method

1. Drop a perpendicular from C and lay off SC to locate S. SC is calculated by the formula

$$SC = \sqrt{V_L C \times CV_R}$$

In most cases S, and in particular V_{45}, will be off the drawing board. Therefore it is preferable to work with one-half $V_L S$, which can be constructed by drawing a perpendicular from $\frac{1}{2}V_L C$ and a horizontal through $\frac{1}{2}SC$. The intersection of both lines marks $\frac{1}{2}V_L S$ (see dotted-line construction in Fig. 3, 4-2).

2. Drop a perpendicular from V_L or from V_R. It is advisable to choose the shorter distance, either $V_L C$ or CV_R.

3. Rotate $V_L S$ or $\frac{1}{2}V_L S$ from V_L downward until intersecting the perpendicular. Mark this point V_{45} or $\frac{1}{2}V_{45}$.

4. Connect this point with the intersection of S_L and A; then continue for locating point A on the vertical at E. This is the equivalent length of A or $\frac{1}{2}A$ upon the vertical at E in the respective perspective.

Note: In Fig. 3, 4-2, it is merely accidental that the projection of the perspective line A intersects exactly at the temporary horizon and at E.

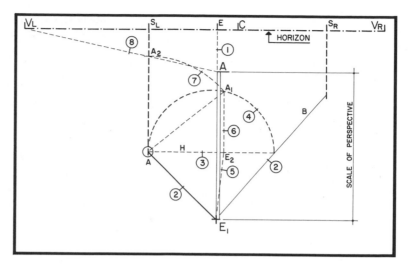

Fig. 3, 4-3

Method 4, Solution c: 90° Turn-up Method

1. After locating the points S_L, E, C, and S_R, drop perpendiculars from S_L and E and locate point E_1 as low as possible.

2. Draw the perspective lines A and B until intersecting the perpendiculars at S_L and S_R.

3. Draw the horizontal H through the intersection of A at S_L or B at S_R, whichever is the shortest, until intersecting the opposite side (see Fig. 3, 4-3).

4. Draw a semicircle over H.

5. Connect E_1 with C to locate E_2 on H.

6. Erect the vertical here to locate A_1 on the semicircle.

7. Transfer A_1 to A_2 on S_L by rotating A_1 from the intersection of A at S_L.

8. Draw the perspective line from V_L through A_2 to locate point A on the vertical at E. The distance from A to E_1 is the equivalent length of side A of the site plan in this perspective. After division into respective sections, it is the scale for the various heights of the object.

METHOD 5: Transfer of Various Heights to Any Point of the Perspective

After the respective scale of a specific perspective has been derived as described in Method 4, Solutions *a–c*, the transfer of various heights to any point of the perspective can be achieved through the following method.

Problem

Transfer the heights h_1, h_2, h_3, and h_4 to the points p_1, p_2, p_3, and p_4.

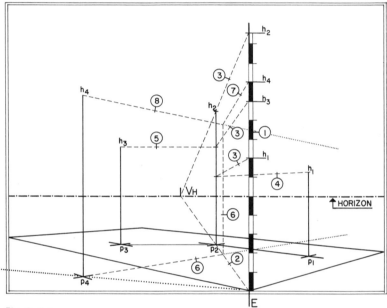

Fig. 3, 5–1

Solution

If two points on the ground plane are on the same perspective line as p_1 and p_2 or on the same line parallel with the horizon as p_2 and p_3 only one vanishing point V_H has to be located.

1. Lay off the heights h_1, h_2, h_3, and h_4 on the vertical measure line at E or on any other vertical in the picture plane conveniently located to the respective points whose heights have to be projected into the perspective.

   In some cases the vertical at E will not be appropriate. The perspective line from E through the respective point to the horizon can be beyond the drawing board, as at point p_4 (see dotted line); therefore another vertical measure line may be more useful.

2. Draw the perspective line from E through p_2 to locate the vanishing point V_H on the horizon.

3. Draw perspective lines from h_1, h_2, and h_3 to V_H to project the heights of p_1, p_2, and p_3 upon the vertical at p_2.

4. Since p_1 and p_2 are on the same perspective line pointing toward V_L, draw the perspective line from V_L through h_1 at the vertical of p_2 to locate h_1 upon the vertical at p_1.

5. p_3 is on the same line as p_2 parallel to the horizon; therefore draw a parallel to the horizon through h_3 toward the vertical

at p_3 to locate h_3 upon that vertical. The height h_2 of p_2 has already been projected in step 3.

6. The vanishing point of the perspective line from E through p_4 is beyond the drawing board; therefore a second vertical measure line conveniently located to p_4 could be erected. In Fig. 3, 5-1 a perspective line was drawn from p_4, converging at V_R and intersecting EV_H. Erect a vertical here.

7. Project upon this vertical h_4 by drawing the perspective line from h_4 at the vertical of E to V_H.

8. Draw the perspective line from V_R through h_4 upon this vertical to project h_4 upon the vertical at p_4.

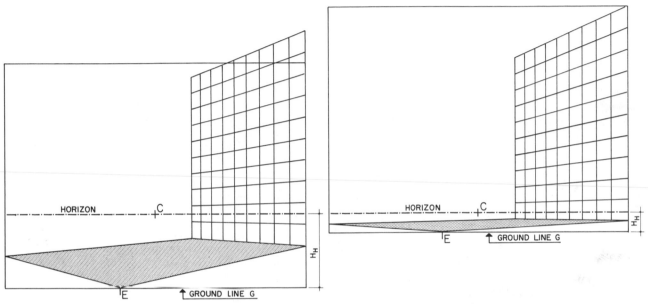

Fig. 3, 6-1

METHOD 6: P_H Projection, the Width of the Perspective Derived from the Excessive Height of the Object

In many cases a readjustment of the size of the perspective is not necessary because an alteration of the level of the ground plane can bring the projection of the object into the frame of the perspective (see Fig. 3, 6-1). Here the height of the horizon H_H has been lowered by raising the level of the ground plane. This minor correction is not appropriate for very high objects.

As Fig. 3, 6-1 shows, the height of the object is approximately three-fourths its width, which is the common setup of the $P_{\max}$ projection. If, however, the size of the object is in the inverse ratio $4:3$, then the height becomes the determinant factor for deriving the width and height of the perspective, and the P_H projection is required.

Very high objects projected from a far distance may not affect the common ratio of height:width $= 3:4$. However, to ascertain whether the object exceeds the normal ratio $3:4$, more information has to be obtained from the site plan.

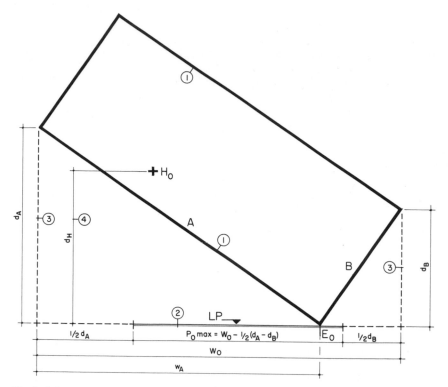

Fig. 3, 6-2

Preparation of the Site Plan

1. Enclose that part of the object to be illustrated by the rectangle *AB*.

2. Draw the straight line *LP* through the foremost corner E_o to establish the angle of position at which the object is to be seen.

3. Drop the perpendiculars d_A and d_B from the left and right corners of *AB* upon *LP* and measure to the scale of the site plan the distance W_o between d_A and d_B and the length of the perpendiculars d_A and d_B.

4. Deduct one-half of the distance d_H between *X* and *LP* from the height H_o of the object at *X* in order to obtain the projected height H_p of H_o upon the picture plane, i.e.,

$$H_o - \tfrac{1}{2}d_H = H_p$$

Determine the height of the horizon H_H, which should not exceed $\tfrac{1}{3}H_p$; then deduct H_H from H_p to obtain $\tfrac{1}{2}SC_o$, which is one-half of the distance between *LP* and the station point *S* in the site plan, i.e.,

$$H_p - H_H = \tfrac{1}{2}SC_o$$
$$SC_o = 2(H_p - H_H)$$

5. In order to obtain the maximum width $P_{\max}$ of the perspective in the site plan, deduct $\tfrac{1}{2}(d_A + d_B)$ from W_o (see step 3); i.e.,

$$P_{o,\max} = W_o - \tfrac{1}{2}(d_A + d_B)$$

Note: If $SC_o \leqq P_{o,\max}$, then the construction can be continued according to the general formula for $P_{\max} = SC$ as quoted in CHARACTERISTICS of the respective methods in Chaps. 1 and 2. If, however, SC_o exceeds $P_{o,\max}$ by more than 10 percent, the construction of the perspective has to be done as follows.

P_H Projection

1. Draw a horizon at a convenient height across the drawing board and locate the vanishing points V_L and V_R. Scale off in inches the distance T between V_L and V_R.

   Derive SC, the distance between the station point S and the center C of the perspective, by the formula

   $$SC = \frac{T}{w_A/d_A + d_A/w_A}$$

   (see Fig. 3, 6-2).

   $\frac{1}{2}SC$ represents the radius of the circle of undistorted projection. For SC in the 45° and 30°/60° perspectives, see Chap. 1, Methods 4 and 5. For the dimensions of d_A and w_A see PREPARATION OF THE SITE PLAN, step 3, page 120.

2. Locate the center C of the perspective by the formulas

   $$V_L C = \frac{w_A}{d_A} SC$$

   $$C V_R = \frac{d_A}{w_A} SC$$

   The calculation is correct if $V_L C$ plus $C V_R$ add to T.

3. Derive the width P_H of the perspective by the formula

   $$\frac{1}{2}P_H = \frac{T}{d_A + 2SC_o + w_A} SC$$

   For the dimension of SC_o see PREPARATION OF THE SITE PLAN, step 4.

   Lay off $\frac{1}{2}P_H$ to the left and right of C, locating S_L and S_R. Erect verticals here, which are the sidelines of the perspective. The distance between S_L and S_R is P_H.

   Note: The point E at which the rectangle AB touches the picture plane has to be located in order to lay out properly the rectangle AB in perspective (see next method, Method 7).

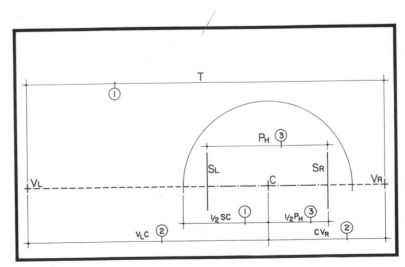

Fig. 3, 6-3

METHOD 7: Determination of the Location of Point E by Computation and Construction

To construct the perspective in accordance with the proportion of AB and its position to the picture plane, it is essential to determine properly the location of point E at which the corner of AB touches the picture plane (see Fig. 3, 7-1).

P_{max} Projection (computation)

Locate point E by the following formula:

$$S_L E = \frac{(A/B)(d_A/w_A)(V_L S_L / S_R V_R)}{[(A/B)(d_A/w_A)(V_L S_L / S_R V_R)] + 1} P_{max}$$

The dimensions of A, B, d_A, and w_A have to be scaled off in the site plan (see Fig. 3, 7-1); the dimensions of $V_L S_L$ and $S_R V_R$ must be taken from the construction of the perspective (see Fig. 3, 7-2). Set up the ratios of the equation as shown above.

Note: A 12-in. slide ruler can be used for the solution of the equation.

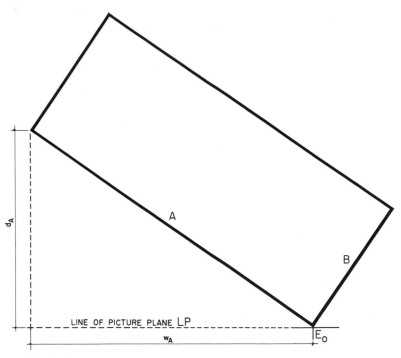

Fig. 3, 7-1

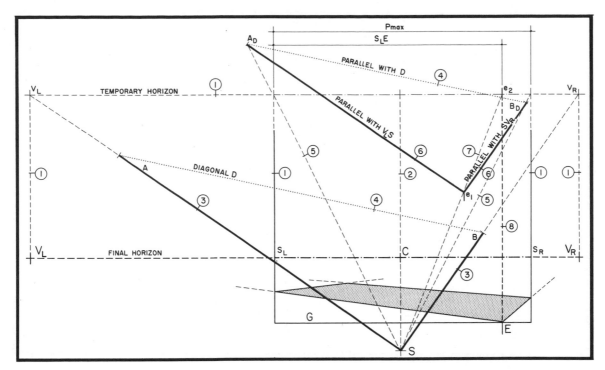

Fig. 3, 7-2

P_{max} **Projection (construction)**

1. Draw a temporary horizon above the final horizon high enough that a perpendicular at C with the length of SC still remains on the drawing board. Transfer V_L, S_L, C, and V_R by erecting verticals at the corresponding points of the final horizon.

2. Drop a perpendicular at C and scale off SC from the temporary horizon to locate S.

3. Connect S with V_L and V_R and lay out the rectangle AB along V_LS and SV_R in any scale.

4. Draw the diagonal D through AB and parallel with it a line above the temporary horizon.

5. Connect S with S_L and S_R at the temporary horizon, intersecting the parallel with D in order to locate A_D and B_D.

6. Draw parallels to V_LS and SV_R through A_D and B_D in order to locate e_1 at their intersection.

7. Connect S with e_1 and continue to intersect the temporary horizon at e_2.

8. Drop a perpendicular from e_2 upon the groundline G to locate point E.

   By connecting E with V_L and V_R on the final horizon to intersect at S_L and S_R, the first two perspective lines of AB are drawn. Drawing a second pair of perspective lines from S_L to V_R and from S_R to V_L completes the perspective layout of AB.

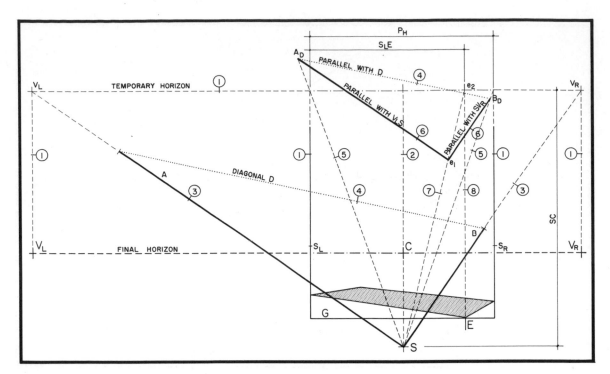

Fig. 3, 7-3

P_H Projection (computation)

Locate point E by the following formula:

$$S_L E = \frac{(A/B)(d_A/w_A)(V_L S_L / S_R V_R)}{[(A/B)(d_A/w_A)(V_L S_L / S_R V_R)] + 1} \, P_H$$

Scale off the dimensions of A, B, d_A, and w_A in the site plan (see Fig. 3, 7-1) and the dimensions of $V_L S_L$ and $S_R V_R$ in the construction of the perspective (see Fig. 3, 7-3). P_H has to be derived according to the P_H PROJECTION, step 3, page 121.

Set up the ratios of the equation as shown above.

P_H Projection (construction)

Follow step by step the instructions for the $P_{\max}$ PROJECTION.

METHOD 8: How to Draw Perspective Lines to a Distant Vanishing Point V_f

This problem consists of two parts:

a. To draw perspective lines upon a vertical plane whose ground-line is the line L_1

b. To draw perspective lines upon a horizontal plane

Problem a

Draw the perspective line L_2 through point P_1, converging at a distant vanishing point V_f of line L_1.

Solution

1. Drop a perpendicular from point P_1 to locate F_1 on the perspective line L_1.
2. Erect the vertical measure line M_v at any point of the ground-line G conveniently located to set up a pair of vanishing points V_1 and V_2, as shown in Fig. 3, 8-1.
3. Draw from M_v at G a line through F_1 in order to locate the first vanishing point V_1 at the horizon.
4. Draw a perspective line from V_1 through P_1 and continue until intersecting M_v at J.
5. Determine the location of the second vanishing point V_2 at the horizon and draw from here a perspective line to M_v at G intersecting L_1 at F_2.
6. Erect a vertical at F_2.
7. Draw a perspective line from V_2 to J in order to locate P_2 at the vertical of F_2.
8. Connect P_1 and P_2 by the line L_2, which is the perspective line in question, converging at the distant vanishing point V_f of L_1.

Note: If intermediate perspective lines are required, divide the vertical M_v between J and G to equivalent spacing desired between L_1 and L_2 (see Fig. 3, 1-2 and text). Transfer this spacing to the verticals at F_1 and F_2 by drawing perspective lines to V_1 and V_2.

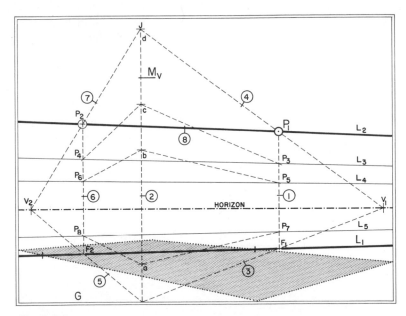

Fig. 3, 8-1

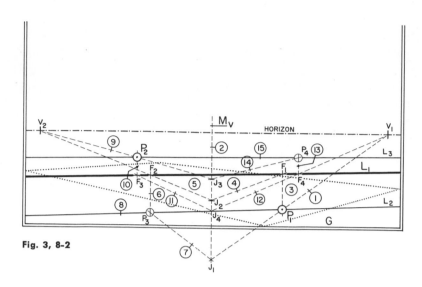

Fig. 3, 8-2

Problem *b*

Draw perspective lines through P_1 and P_2, converging at the distant vanishing point V_f in common with line L_1.

Solution

1. Locate vanishing point V_1 at the horizon and draw the perspective line from V_1 through P_1, continuing until reaching approximately midpoint J_1 between P_1 and P_2.
2. Erect here the vertical measure line M_v.
3. Draw the vertical at P_1 to locate F_1 on L_1.
4. Draw perspective line from F_1 until it intersects M_v at J_2.
5. Locate the second vanishing point V_2 at the horizon and draw the perspective line from J_2 to V_2, intersecting L_1 at F_2.
6. Drop a perpendicular from F_2.
7. Draw the perspective line from J_1 to V_2 until it intersects the perpendicular at F_2 in order to locate P_3.
8. Draw the perspective line through P_1 and P_3, in order that it converge at the distant vanishing point V_f of line L_1.
9. Draw the perspective line from V_2 through P_2 until it intersects M_v at J_3.
10. Drop a perpendicular from P_2 to locate F_3 at L_1.
11. Draw the perspective line from V_2 through F_3 until it intersects M_v to locate J_4.
12. Draw the perspective line from J_4 to V_1 to locate F_4 at L_1.
13. Erect the vertical at F_4.
14. Draw the perspective line from J_3 to V_1 in order to locate P_4 at the vertical of F_4.
15. Draw the perspective line L_3 through P_2 and P_4, in order that it converge at the distant vanishing point of L_1.

Note: Intermediate perspective lines between L_2 and L_3 have to be drawn according to *Note* on the preceding Method 8, Problem *a*, page 125. The more meticulously this projection is done, the more accurate the result will be.

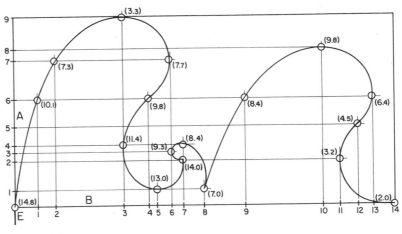

Fig. 3, 9-1

METHOD 9: Curves in Perspective

Four categories of curves have to be distinguished:
1. The regular planimetric curves (circle, parabola, ellipse)
2. The irregular planimetric curves (bent lines without any consistency of inflection)
3. The regular stereometric curves (cylindric spiral, spheric spiral, serpentine)
4. The irregular stereometric curves (bent lines without any consistency of inflection in width and height)

For the purpose of drawing perspective curves, it is sufficient to group them into two categories, the planimetric curves and the stereometric curves. All curves, whether planimetric or stereometric, regular or irregular, must first be laid out in plan like any other object. One similarity exists among all these plans: the characteristic points of the curve must be related to the two sides *A* and *B* of an enclosed rectangle (see Fig. 3, 9-1).

Stereometric curves need an additional determination in height. If the plan of a curve gives full information of its various heights, it then becomes unnecessary to draw a side elevation of that curve. The plan of the curve with its marked heights (see Fig. 3, 9-1, numbers in parentheses) and the perspective of this plan are the two essential components.

It is easy to conceive how a circle or a ball appears in perspective. However, visualizing a picture of an irregular stereometric curve in perspective will be a challenge for the most experienced freehand perspective designer, and the results of even the expert may still be questionable. If enough time and money are at hand, then a model is the best solution. Otherwise, the construction of a perspective based on plan and elevation will be the final time and money saver. Furthermore, a perspective drawing remains the only way to describe a planned object, an object not yet in existence.

Four problems and their solutions will be presented in the following instructions.

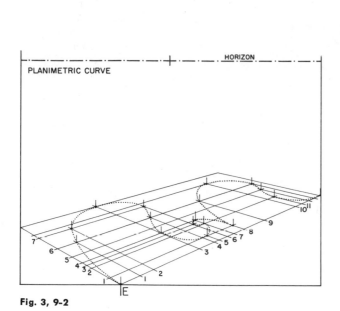

PLANIMETRIC CURVE

HORIZON

Fig. 3, 9-2

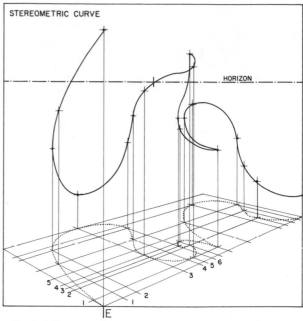

STEREOMETRIC CURVE

HORIZON

Fig. 3, 9-3

Problem a

Project the plan of the spiral staircase, as shown in Fig. 3, 9-4, into perspective.

Note: The size of the perspective and the vanishing points have been established by Method 1 in Chap. 2 (see Fig. 2, 1-3), because the height of the object obviously exceeded the circle of undistorted projection. The rectangle AB, in this case a square, has already been drawn in perspective (see Fig. 3, 9-5).

Solution

1. After enclosing the circle of the stair by the rectangle AB, draw through each point of the outer circle one parallel to A and one to B. Mark them consecutively (see Fig. 3, 9-4).
2. Divide side A proportionally in accordance with the instruction in Chap. 3, Method 2 (see Fig. 3, 9-5).
3. Apply the same method to divide side B.

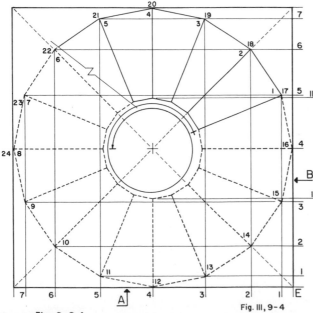

Fig. 3, 9-4

Fig. III, 9-4

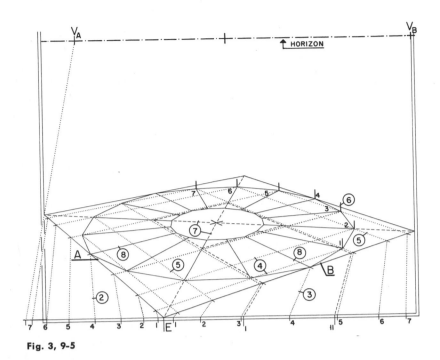

Fig. 3, 9-5

4. Draw perspective lines from each point of side A to the vanishing point V_R.
5. Apply the same procedure to the points at side B by using the vanishing point V_L.
6. Mark the intersections of the parallels according to Fig. 3, 9-4.
7. Draw diagonals of the rectangle to locate the center of the staircase.
8. Connect each marked intersection with the center of the staircase.
9. Connect the marks of side B with the center of the staircase (compare Fig. 3, 9-5 with Fig. 3, 9-6) in order to project them perspectively upon the inner side B and draw perspective lines from them to V_L.

Where these perspective lines intersect the radial lines of the center the corresponding points of the outer circle are projected upon the inner circle.

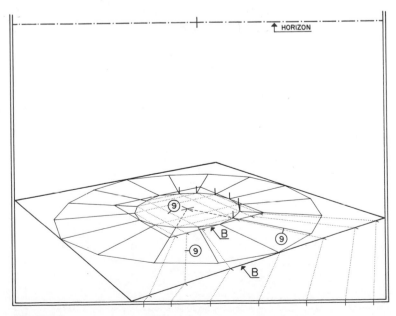

Fig. 3, 9-6

Project the spiral staircase, as laid out in plan, in full height, as demonstrated in Fig. 3, 9-7a.

Note: The height of the staircase measuring 12 ft or 24 risers as well as the height of the horizon set at 6 ft has already been taken in consideration by the determination of the size of the perspective. Height and distance from step to step are also known to equal 6 in. Therefore, it is not necessary to draw a side elevation of the spiral staircase.

Solution

1. See Fig. 3, 9-7a. Erect the vertical at *E* in order to intersect the horizon. Taking the distance from the horizon to *E* as 6 ft, measure to this scale 12 ft from *E* upward to locate the full height of the stair. Divide this full height in as many equal sections as there are steps in the spiral stair, i.e., 24 risers.

2. Erect the vertical at the center of the staircase, draw the connecting line from *E* through the center, and continue in order to locate V_6 at the horizon. Transfer the sections of the divided vertical at *E* to the center vertical by drawing perspective lines from each section to V_6.

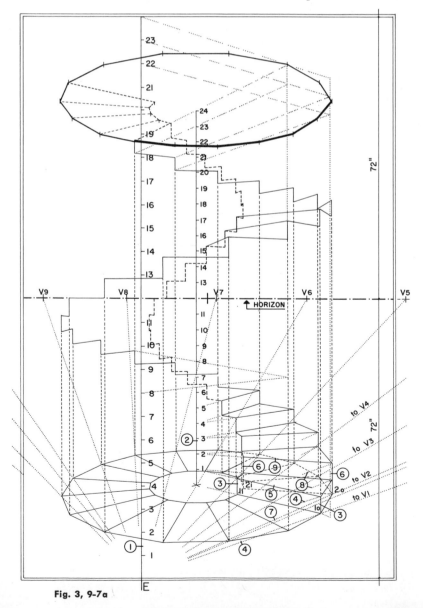

Fig. 3, 9-7a

3. Erect verticals at 1_o and 1_i (first riser).
4. Connect E with 1_o and continue until locating V_1 at the horizon. Transfer the height of the first section at E to 1_o by drawing a perspective line from E_1 to V_1.
5. Connect the height of 1_o with the first section of the center vertical in order to determine the height of the first riser at the vertical of 1_i. This completes the picture of the first riser in perspective.
6. Erect verticals at 2_o and 2_i (second riser).
7. Draw the connecting line from E through 2_o and continue in order to locate V_2 at the horizon.
8. Draw perspective lines from E_1 and E_2 to V_2 in order to locate the height of 1_o and 2_o at the vertical of 2_o.
9. Connect the height of 1_o and 2_o at the vertical of 2_o with section 1 and 2 of the center vertical to locate the height of the first and second risers at the vertical of 2_i.
10. Erect verticals at 3_o and 3_i (third riser).
11. Draw the connecting line from E through 3_o and continue in order to locate V_3 at the horizon.
12. Draw perspective lines from section 2 and 3 of E to V_3 to locate the height of the second and third risers at the vertical

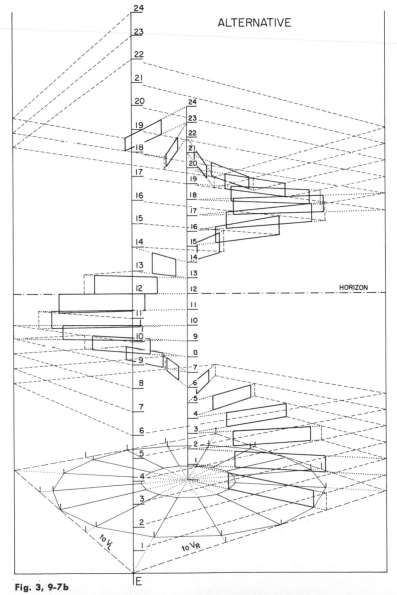

Fig. 3, 9-7b

of 3_o. Continue in the same way until all risers have been located at the verticals of their corresponding points in plan.

Figure 3, 9-7b shows an alternative solution. By using only the vanishing points V_L and V_R the height of each step is projected upon the corresponding vertical at the intersection of a radial line with the outline of AB. Then the height of the step has to be connected with the respective height at the center vertical to outline the riser.

For the completion of the perspective in Fig. 3, 9-7b, the outlines of the inner and outer circle have to be filled in at each riser, as demonstrated in Fig. 3, 9-8. If a railing has to be added at the thickness of the spiral slab, use separately the height of each riser in perspective as a measuring unit to determine the height of the railing at that point.

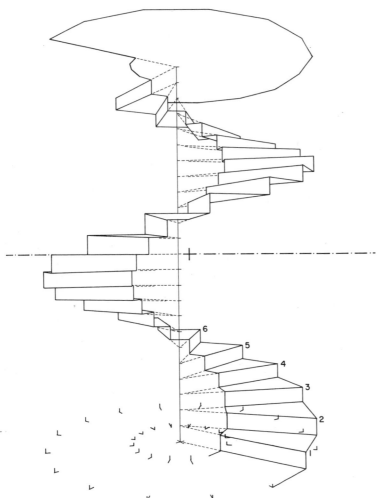

Fig. 3, 9-8

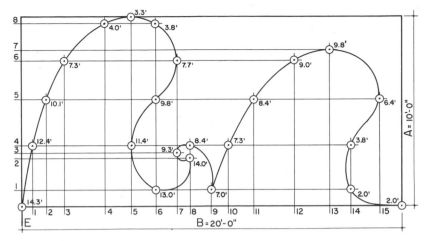

Fig. 3, 9-9

Problem c

Draw the plan of an irregular curve in perspective as laid out in plan (see Fig. 3, 9-9).

Note: The size of the perspective and the vanishing points have been determined by the instructions in Chap. 2, Method 1. The rectangle *AB* has already been drawn (see Fig. 3, 9-10).

Solution

1. Enclose the curve by the rectangle $AB = 10 \times 20$ ft and draw a grid through the characteristic points of the curve to relate them to the sides *A* and *B*. Number each intersection consecutively (see Fig. 3, 9-9).

2. Project the sections of side *A* upon the perspective line *A* by applying Method 2 in Chap. 3 (see Fig. 3, 2-1). Then draw perspective lines from each projected section to the vanishing point V_R.

3. Apply the same method to project the sections of side *B* upon the perspective line *B* and draw perspective lines to V_L.

4. Number correspondingly the intersections (see Fig. 3, 9-10) according to the grid in Fig. 3, 9-9. Connect the points to an even curve, thus completing the drawing of the irregular curve of Fig. 3, 9-9 in perspective.

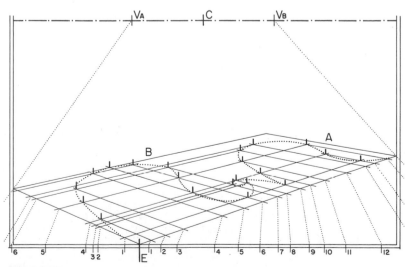

Fig. 3, 9-10

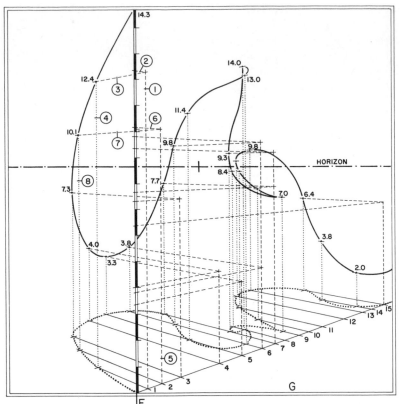

Fig. 3, 9-11

Problem d

Draw the irregular curve as laid out in Fig. 3, 9-9 stereometrically in perspective.

Note: The plan of this curve has a series of points with numbers indicating the level of this specific point above the ground plane. The horizon is 8.6′ above the ground plane according to the scale of the perspective, which has been derived as described in Chap. 3, Method 4, Solution *c* in accordance with Chap. 2, Method 1 (see Fig. 2, 1-3). Figure 3, 9-10 shows this curve in perspective.

Solution

1. Erect a vertical at the first section of side *B* marked by a perspective line from V_L through the first point of the curve.
2. Transfer the respective height of this point from the vertical measure line at *E* by drawing a perspective line to V_R intersecting that vertical.

3. Draw a perspective line from this projected height to V_L.
4. Erect a vertical at the first point of the curve in order to intersect the transferring line from the first vertical. Thus the first point of the curve has been located.
5. Erect a vertical at the second section of B, transfer the respective height of this point from the vertical measure line at E by a perspective line to V_R, and continue according to steps 3 and 4, locating the second point of the curve in perspective. See circled numbers 5, 6, 7, 8 in Fig. 3, 9-11.

After projecting each point into perspective, complete the stereometric curve by drawing an even curve from point to point.

Note: This curve on a flat piece of paper does not give any information about its three-dimensional appearance unless the designer adds specific features by illustrative means (see Fig. 3, 9-12).

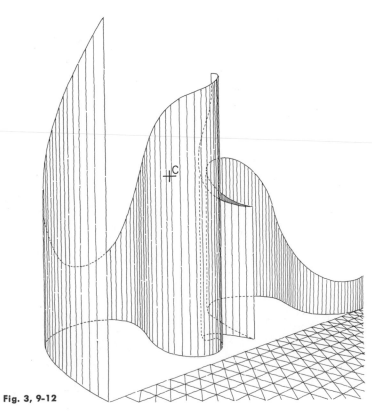

Fig. 3, 9-12

APPENDIX

Derivation of the Applied Formulas

Principle of the Right Triangle

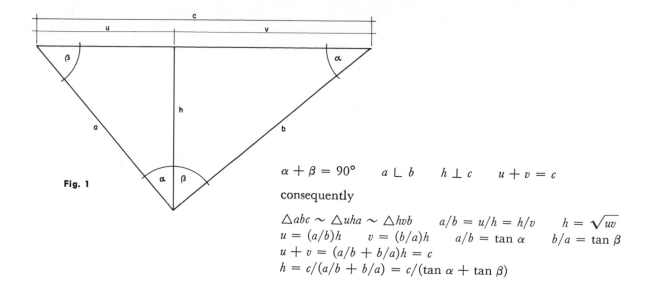

Fig. 1

$$\alpha + \beta = 90° \qquad a \perp b \qquad h \perp c \qquad u + v = c$$

consequently

$$\triangle abc \sim \triangle uha \sim \triangle hvb \qquad a/b = u/h = h/v \qquad h = \sqrt{uv}$$
$$u = (a/b)h \qquad v = (b/a)h \qquad a/b = \tan \alpha \qquad b/a = \tan \beta$$
$$u + v = (a/b + b/a)h = c$$
$$h = c/(a/b + b/a) = c/(\tan \alpha + \tan \beta)$$

Application to the Perspective Construction

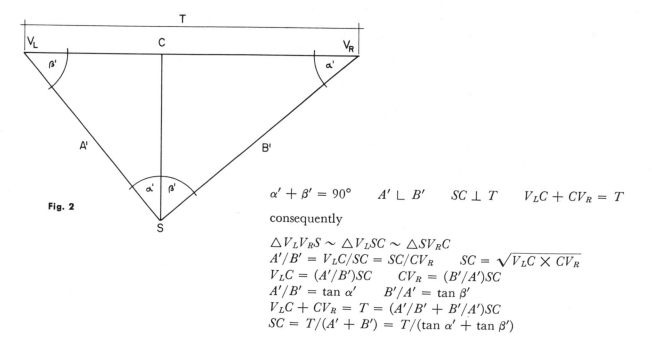

Fig. 2

$$\alpha' + \beta' = 90° \qquad A' \perp B' \qquad SC \perp T \qquad V_L C + C V_R = T$$

consequently

$$\triangle V_L V_R S \sim \triangle V_L S C \sim \triangle S V_R C$$
$$A'/B' = V_L C/SC = SC/CV_R \qquad SC = \sqrt{V_L C \times CV_R}$$
$$V_L C = (A'/B')SC \qquad CV_R = (B'/A')SC$$
$$A'/B' = \tan \alpha' \qquad B'/A' = \tan \beta'$$
$$V_L C + CV_R = T = (A'/B' + B'/A')SC$$
$$SC = T/(A' + B') = T/(\tan \alpha' + \tan \beta')$$

Determination and Application of the Main Line of Sight SC to locate the center C of the perspective when the diagonal D of the rectangle AB is parallel with the picture plane LP

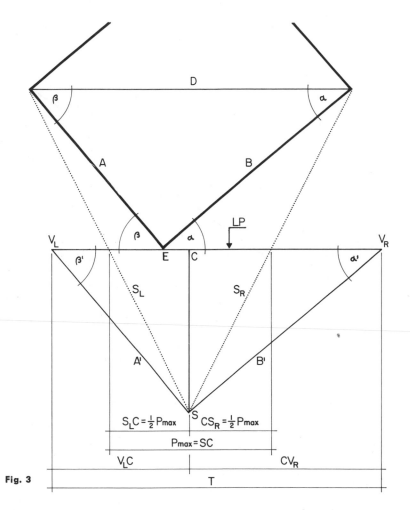

Fig. 3

$\alpha + \beta = 90°$ $\alpha = \alpha'$ $\beta = \beta'$
$A \parallel A'$ $B \parallel B'$ $D \parallel LP \parallel T$

consequently

$\triangle ABD \sim \triangle A'B'T$ $A'/B' = A/B = \tan \alpha$
$$B'/A' = B/A = \tan \beta$$
$SC = T/(\tan \alpha + \tan \beta) = T/(A/B + B/A)$
$S_LC = CS_R = \frac{1}{2}SC = \frac{1}{2}P_{max}$
$V_LC = (A/B)SC = (A/B)P_{max}$
$CV_R = (B/A)SC = (B/A)P_{max}$

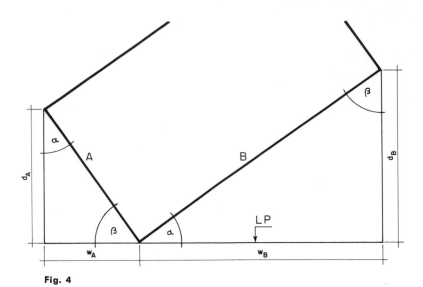

Fig. 4

Site Plan Diagram

$$\alpha + \beta = 90° \qquad A \sqsubset B \qquad d_A \perp LP \qquad d_B \perp LP$$

consequently

$$\triangle A d_A w_A \sim \triangle B w_B d_B$$
$$\alpha' + \beta' = 90° \qquad \alpha' = \alpha \qquad \beta' = \beta \qquad A' \sqsubset B' \qquad SC \perp T$$

consequently

$$\triangle A d_A w_A \sim \triangle SCV_L \sim \triangle B w_B d_B \sim \triangle V_R CS$$
$$V_L C/SC = w_A/d_A \qquad V_L C = (w_A/d_A)SC$$
$$CV_R/SC = d_A/w_A \qquad CV_R = (d_A/w_A)SC$$
$$V_L C + CV_R = (w_A/d_A + d_A/w_A)SC = T$$
$$SC = T/(w_A/d_A + d_A/w_A)$$

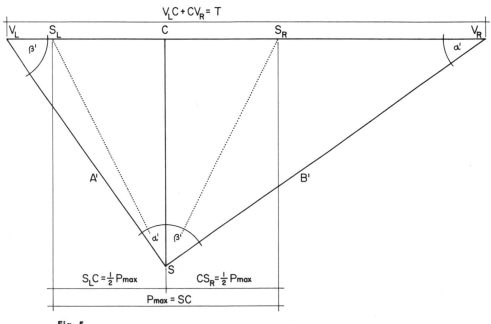

Fig. 5

Determination of the Main Line of Sight SC when the center C of the perspective is determined by the designer

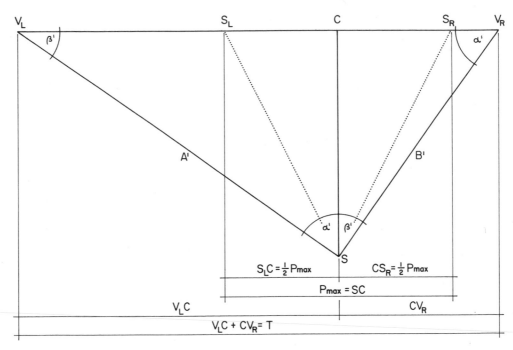

Fig. 6

$\alpha' + \beta' = 90°$ $A' \llcorner B'$ $SC \perp T$

consequently

$\triangle A'B'T \sim \triangle V_L CS \sim \triangle SCV_R$

$A'/B' = V_L C/SC = SC/CV_R$ $(SC)^2 = V_L C \times CV_R$

$SC = \sqrt{V_L C \times CV_R} = P_{\max}$ $S_L C = CS_R = \frac{1}{2}P_{\max} = \frac{1}{2}SC$

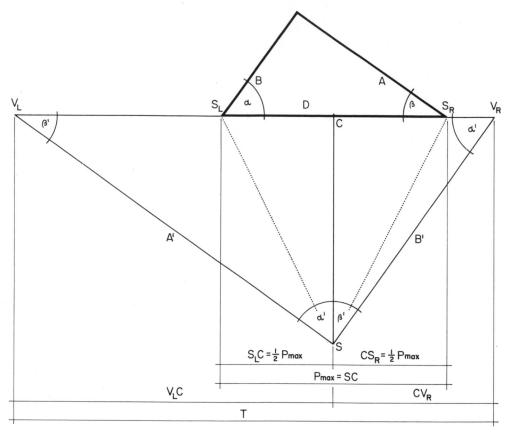

Fig. 7

$$A/B < 2 \qquad A/B > \tfrac{1}{2} \qquad \alpha + \beta = 90°$$
$$A' \parallel A \qquad B' \parallel B \qquad A \perp B \qquad A' \perp B'$$

consequently

$$\triangle A'B'T \sim \triangle ABD \sim \triangle V_L CS \sim \triangle SCV_R$$
$$A'/B' = A/B = V_L C/SC = SC/CV_R$$
$$V_L C = (A/B)SC \qquad CV_R = (B/A)SC$$
$$V_L C + CV_R = T = (A/B + B/A)SC$$
$$SC = T/(A/B + B/A) = P_{\max}$$

Determination and Application of the Main Line of Sight SC when the diagonal D of the rectangle AB is the picture plane LP and the ratio A:B is more than 2 or less than ½ (Re: Method 1, 3b)

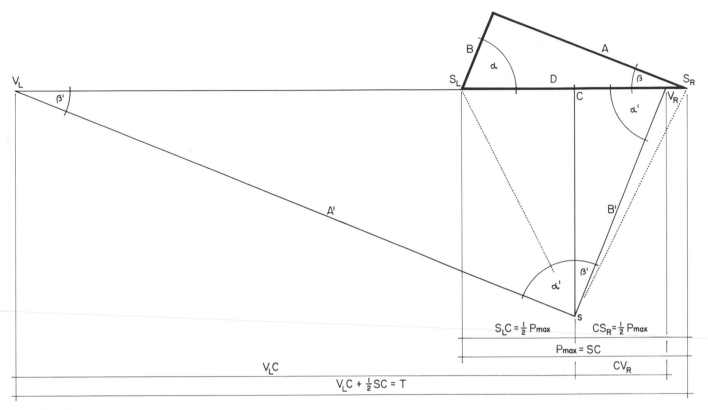

Fig. 8

$A/B > 2 \quad$ or $\quad A/B < \frac{1}{2} \quad \alpha + \beta = 90°$

$A' \parallel A \quad B' \parallel B \quad A \llcorner B \quad A' \llcorner B' \quad SC \perp T$

consequently

$\triangle A'B'T \sim \triangle ABD \sim \triangle V_L SC \sim \triangle V_R SC$

$A'/B' = A/B = V_L C/SC = SC/CV_R$

$V_L C = (A/B)SC \qquad CV_R = (B/A)SC$

$S_L C = CS_R = \frac{1}{2}D = \frac{1}{2}SC = \frac{1}{2}P_{max}$

$V_L C + CS_R = T = (A/B + \frac{1}{2})SC$

$SC = T/(A/B + \frac{1}{2}) = P_{max}$

If the ratio $A:B$ is less than $\frac{1}{2}$, the formula changes to

$$SC = \frac{T}{\frac{1}{2} + B/A} = P_{max}$$

which means V_L moves between S_L and C and V_R beyond S_R.

*Method 1, 6 designates Method 6 in Chapter 1.

The Circle of Undistorted Projection

To be correct, it should be called *the circle of less distorted projection*, because every projection upon a flat surface is somewhat distorted, depending on the width of the angle of sight. Only a projection upon a convex surface whose focus is the station point S is actually undistorted. The diameter of that circle, taken as the maximum width P_{max} of the perspective, and the distance between the station point S and the center C of the perspective are equated for practical reasons in this book, i.e.,

$$P_{max} = SC$$

Consequently, the ratio of $\frac{1}{2}P_{max}$ to SC is $\frac{1}{2}$, which is the tangent of the angle σ (sigma) of $\approx 26°30'$. Therefore, the left and the right sidelines S_L and S_R of the sector of vision form an angle of about 53°. P_{max} is the maximum possible width of the projected object on the drawing board.

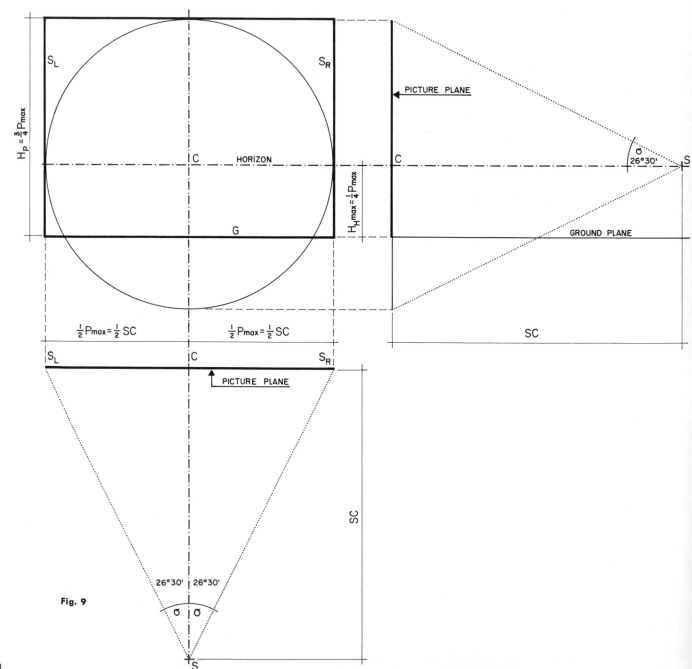

Fig. 9

144

$P_{o,\max}$—not to be confused with $P_{\max}$—is the maximum width of the projected object upon the picture plane LP in the site plan. Its value is only of theoretical importance in determining when to use the P_H projection for high objects.

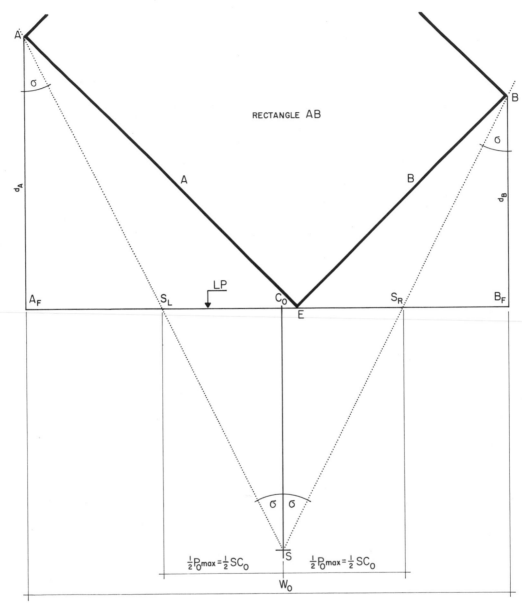

Fig. 10

d_A, SC_o, and $d_B \perp LP$ SC_o bisecting $\angle ASB$

consequently

$\triangle AS_L A_F \sim SC_o S_L \sim \triangle BS_R B_F \sim \triangle SC_o S_R$

$\triangle SC_o S_L \cong \triangle SC_o S_R$ $S_L C_o = C_o S_R = \frac{1}{2} SC_o = \frac{1}{2} P_{o,\max}$

$A_F S_L / d_A = S_L C_o / SC_o = C_o S_R / SC_o = S_R B_F / d_B = \frac{1}{2}$

therefore

$A_F S_L = \frac{1}{2} d_A$ $S_R B_F = \frac{1}{2} d_B$ $A_F C_o + C_o B_F = W_o$

$W_o - \frac{1}{2}(d_A + d_B) = P_{o,\max}$

SC_o—not to be confused with SC—is the distance between the station point S and the center C_o of the projected object upon LP in the site plan. Here again, its value is necessary only for comparison with the value of $P_{o,\max}$ in order to derive P_H, the width of the perspective for high objects.

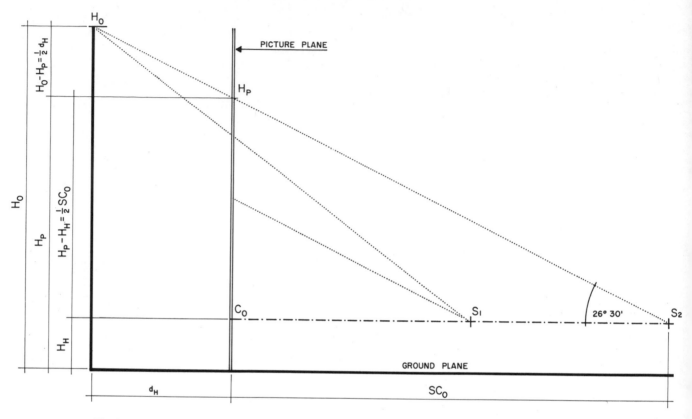

Fig. 11

SC_o is determined by the height of the object H_o and the angle σ (sigma), $\approx 26°30'$. If the observer, for instance, focuses on the top of the high object H_o from the station point S_1, the angle is obviously wider than at S_2, which results in distortions in the upper part of the perspective.

To avoid these distortions, the observer has to step back to the station point S_2 in order to lower the line of sight to the required maximum angle of $26°30'$. That means the distance between S_2 and C_o—called in short SC_o—has to be increased until SC_o equals two times the height H_p of the projected object upon the picture plane minus two times the height of the horizon H_H; i.e.,

$$SC_o = 2(H_p - H_H)$$

or

$$\frac{H_p - H_H}{SC_o} = \frac{1}{2}$$

which is the tangent of $\angle \sigma$ (sigma).

The same ratio applies to the relation of the height of the object H_o, minus its projection H_p upon the picture plane, to the distance d_H of the object from the picture plane; i.e.,

$$\frac{H_o - H_p}{d_H} = \frac{1}{2}$$

or

$$H_p = H_o - \tfrac{1}{2}d_H$$

It is a general rule that the height H_H of the horizon in a perspective with common eye level should not exceed $\tfrac{1}{4}P_{max}$, i.e.,

$$H_{H,max} = \tfrac{1}{4}P_{o,max}$$

Consequently

$$SC_o = 2(H_p - H_H) = 2H_p - \tfrac{1}{2}P_{o,max} = 2H_o - (d_H + \tfrac{1}{2}P_{o,max})$$

The height of the object H_o is known.

The distance d_H of the object from the picture plane has to be scaled off in the site plan after the position of the rectangle AB to the picture plane has been established. At that stage the height of the horizon H_H should also be determined.

If SC_o exceeds $P_{o,\max}$, especially if the high object is near the sidelines S_L and S_R and is close to a vanishing point, the P_H projection is necessary to avoid right angles at the top and bottom of a right-angled object.

As soon as a right angle or, worst of all, an acute angle appears in the perspective of a right-angled object with the two vanishing points beyond the sidelines, opening its sides either to the background or to the foreground, the perspective is distorted, as shown in Fig. 12. This natural fact cannot be altered despite correct construction of a perspective.

There are no limits to what can be illustrated in a perspective projection, but this does not ensure that a projection will be a true reflection of what is seen in reality.

A right angle appears there, as such, only where its sides are parallel with the picture plane. If, however, a right angle is part of a plane parallel with the ground plane moving away from the station point toward the horizon, then it flattens more and more, becoming an obtuse angle but never a right or even an acute one.

The circle of absolute distortion spans over $V_L V_R = T$, and on the picture plane it is the *Locus Geometricus* for an infinite number of apexes of the right angles over the base T. The top of the object must be drawn below that circle. The more the object approaches V_L or V_R, the less height is left to be projected without distortion (see Fig. 12 above $V_L V_R$). On the horizontal plane at eye level the circle of absolute distortion is the *Locus Geometricus* for an infinite number of station points determining the length of SC. Here again, the closer the center of the perspective comes to a vanishing point the more $SC = P_{\max}$ decreases, which defines the circle of undistorted projection (see Fig. 12 below $V_L V_R$).

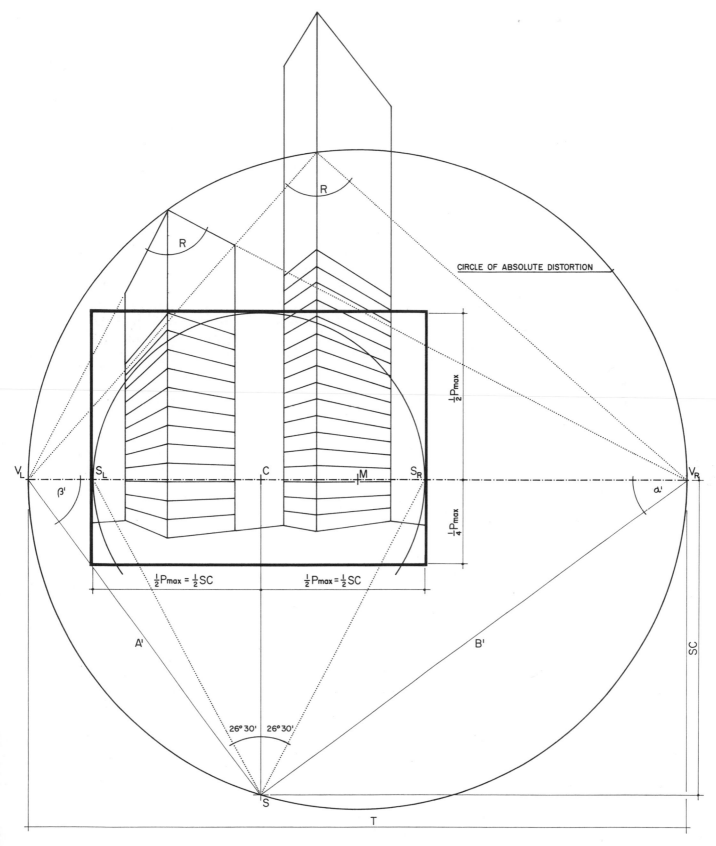

CIRCLE OF ABSOLUTE DISTORTION

Fig. 12

149

Determination of P_H

P_H is the maximal width of a perspective derived from the height of a high object.

(Re: Method 1, 2, 3a, 3b, 6)

An object is considered to be high when the factor SC_o exceeds the factor $P_{o,\max}$ (see pages 144–147).

$$AC_A \parallel C_B B \parallel LP \qquad SC_o \perp LP \qquad S_L C_o = C_o S_R$$
$$\angle \sigma = \angle \sigma' \qquad SC \perp S_L S_R \qquad S_L C = CS_R$$

consequently

$$\triangle SCS_L \cong \triangle SCS_R \qquad \triangle SC_A A \sim \triangle SC_B B \sim \triangle SCS_L \sim \triangle SCS_R$$
$$AC_A/(d_A + SC_o) = BC_B/(d_B + SC_o) = S_L C/SC = CS_R/SC$$
$$AC_A = (S_L C/SC)(d_A + SC_o) \qquad BC_B = (S_L C/SC)(d_B + SC_o)$$
$$AC_A + BC_B = (S_L C/SC)(d_A + 2SC_o + d_B) = W_o$$
$$S_L C = CS_R = [W_o/(d_A + 2SC_o + d_B)]SC = \tfrac{1}{2}P_H$$

W_o, d_A, and d_B have to be scaled off in the site plan after the rectangle AB and its position to LP have been established. For SC_o, see page 147; for SC, see pages 139–143 and 153, whichever refers to the employed method.

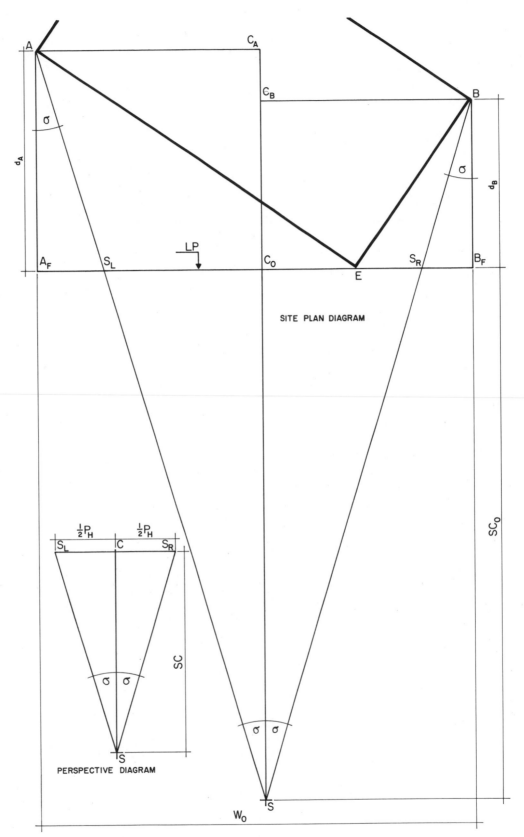

SITE PLAN DIAGRAM

PERSPECTIVE DIAGRAM

Fig. 13

151

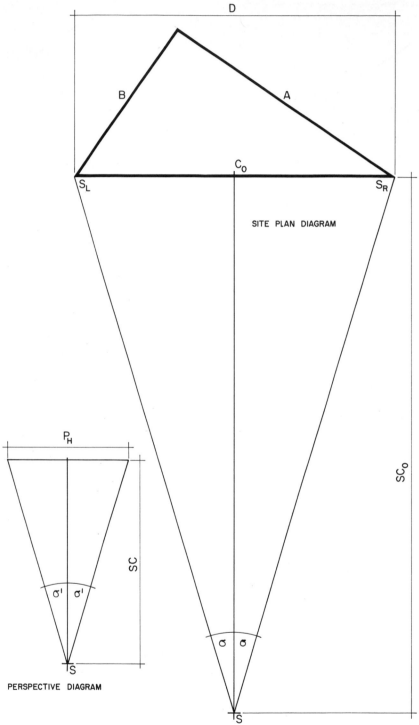

D

B   A

C_o

S_L S_R

SITE PLAN DIAGRAM

SC_o

P_H

SC

σ' σ'

σ σ

S

PERSPECTIVE DIAGRAM

S

Fig. 14

$$SC_o/D = f \qquad A/B < 2 \qquad A/B > \tfrac{1}{2}$$
$$SC_o \perp D \qquad SC \perp P_H \qquad \angle\sigma = \angle\sigma'$$
$$\triangle SC_o S_L \cong \triangle SC_o S_R \qquad \triangle SCS_L \cong \triangle SCS_R$$

consequently

$$SC_o/D = SC/P_H = f \qquad P_H = SC/f$$

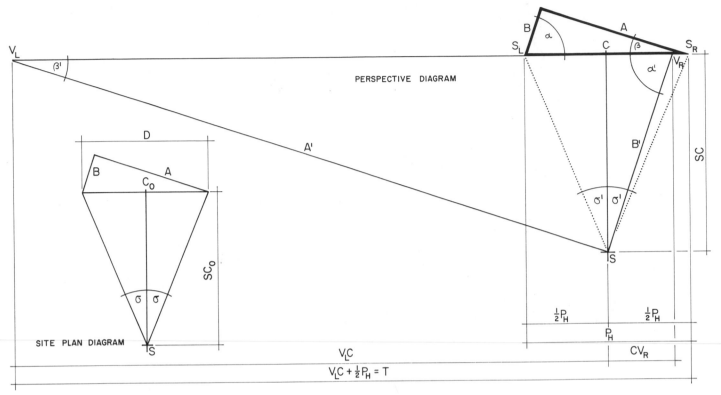

PERSPECTIVE DIAGRAM

SITE PLAN DIAGRAM

$V_L C + \tfrac{1}{2}P_H = T$

Fig. 15

$A/B > 2$ (as shown in Fig. 15)

$V_L C + \tfrac{1}{2}P_H = T \qquad V_L C/SC = A/B \qquad V_L C = (A/B)SC$

$SC/P_H = SC_o/D = f \qquad P_H = SC/f \qquad \tfrac{1}{2}P_H = \tfrac{1}{2}(SC/f)$

$V_L C + \tfrac{1}{2}P_H = \left(A/B + \dfrac{1}{2f}\right)SC = T \qquad SC = T\Big/\left(A/B + \dfrac{1}{2f}\right)$

$A/B < \tfrac{1}{2}$

$\tfrac{1}{2}P_H = CV_R = T \qquad CV_R/SC = B/A \qquad CV_R = (B/A)SC$

$SC/P_H = SC_o/D = f \qquad P_H = SC/f \qquad \tfrac{1}{2}P_H = \tfrac{1}{2}(SC/f)$

$\tfrac{1}{2}P_H + CV_R = \left(\dfrac{1}{2f} + B/A\right)SC = T \qquad SC = T\Big/\left(\dfrac{1}{2f} + B/A\right)$

Note: The application of f in this computation of SC is limited to

$f_{max} = \tfrac{1}{2}(A/B) \qquad$ where $\qquad A/B > 2$

$f_{max} = \tfrac{1}{2}(B/A) \qquad$ where $\qquad A/B < \tfrac{1}{2}$

which means S_R moves closer to C bypassing V_R, or S_L moves closer to C bypassing V_L; therefore T again equals $V_L C$ plus CV_R, which is a plausible result because of the drastic reduction of P_{max} to P_H.

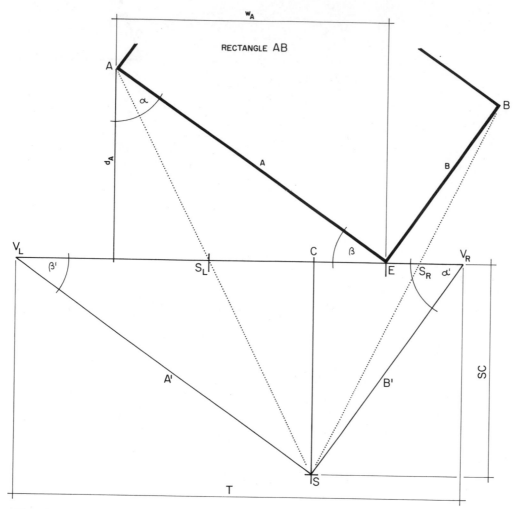

Fig. 16

$\alpha + \beta = 90°$ 　　 $\alpha = \alpha'$ 　　 $\beta = \beta'$ 　　 $A' \parallel A$ 　　 $B' \parallel B$

$A \perp B$ 　　 $A' \perp B'$ 　　 $d_A \perp w_A$

$\triangle A d_A w_A \sim \triangle T B' A' \sim \triangle S C V_L$

$B'/A' = d_A/w_A = SC/V_L C = CV_R/SC$

$\triangle S_L E A \sim \triangle S_L V_L S$ 　　 $\triangle S_R E B \sim \triangle S_R V_R S$

consequently

$S_L E/V_L S_L = A/A'$ 　　 $S_L E = (A/A')V_L S_L$

$ES_R/S_R V_R = B/B'$ 　　 $ES_R = (B/B')S_R V_R$

$S_L E/ES_R = (A/B)(B'/A')(V_L S_L/S_R V_R)$

$$= (A/B)(d_A/w_A)(V_L S_L/S_R V_R)$$

$S_L E/(S_L E + ES_R)$

$$= (A)(d_A)(V_L S_L)/[(A)(d_A)(V_L S_L) + (B)(w_A)(S_R V_R)]$$

$S_L E + ES_R = P_{\max}$ 　　 or 　　 P_H

$$\frac{S_L E}{P_{\max}} = \frac{(A)(d_A)(V_L S_L)}{(A)(d_A)(V_L S_L) + (B)(w_A)(S_R V_R)} \frac{1/(B)(w_A)(S_R V_R)}{1/(B)(w_A)(S_R V_R)}$$

$$S_L E = \frac{(A/B)(d_A/w_A)(V_L S_L/S_R V_R)}{[(A/B)(d_A/w_A)(V_L S_L/S_R V_R)] + 1} P_{\max} \quad \text{or} \quad P_H$$

$SC/V_L C$ or CV_R/SC can be used instead of d_A/w_A.

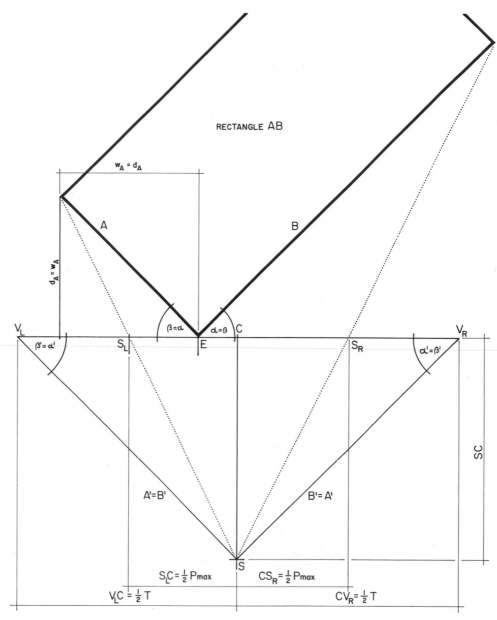

RECTANGLE AB

$w_A = d_A$

$d_A = w_A$

A

B

$\beta = \alpha$

$\alpha = \beta$

C

V_L

$\beta' = \alpha'$

S_L

E

S_R

V_R

$\alpha' = \beta'$

$A' = B'$

$B' = A'$

SC

$\underline{S}$

$S_LC = \frac{1}{2} P_{max}$

$CS_R = \frac{1}{2} P_{max}$

$V_LC = \frac{1}{2} T$

$CV_R = \frac{1}{2} T$

Fig. 17

$$\alpha + \beta = 90° \qquad \alpha = \beta = 45° \qquad \alpha = \alpha' \qquad \beta = \beta'$$
$$A' = B' \qquad V_LC = CV_R = SC \qquad SC/V_LC = CV_R/SC = 1$$
$$d_A \parallel SC \qquad d_A \perp T \qquad SC \perp T \qquad d_A = w_A \qquad d_A/w_A = 1$$
$$S_LC = CS_R \qquad V_LC - S_LC = CV_R - CS_R$$
$$V_LS_L = S_RV_R \qquad V_LS_L/S_RV_R = 1$$

$$S_LE = \frac{(A/B)(d_A/w_A)(V_LS_L/S_RV_R)}{[(A/B)(d_A/w_A)(V_LS_L/S_RV_R)] + 1} \, P_{max} = \frac{A/B}{(A/B) + 1} \, P_{max}$$

$$= \frac{A}{A + B} \, P_{max} \quad \text{or}$$

P_H in the case of a P_H projection.

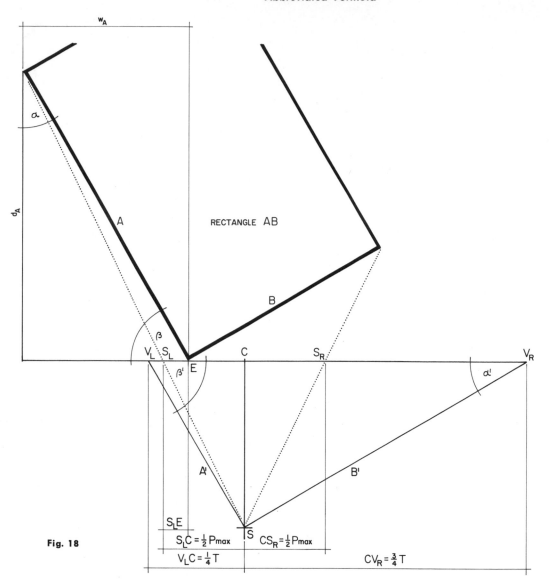

Fig. 18

$$\alpha + \beta = 90° \qquad \alpha = 30° \qquad \beta = 60° \qquad \alpha = \alpha' \qquad \beta = \beta'$$

$$V_L C = \tfrac{1}{4}T \qquad CV_R = \tfrac{3}{4}T \qquad SC = \sqrt{V_L C \times CV_R} = \tfrac{1}{4}T\sqrt{3}$$

$$A' = \tfrac{1}{2}T \qquad B' = \tfrac{1}{2}T\sqrt{3} \qquad B'/A' = SC/V_L C = d_A/w_A = \sqrt{3}$$

$$V_L S_L = V_L C - \tfrac{1}{2}SC = \tfrac{1}{4}T - \tfrac{1}{2}\,\tfrac{1}{4}T\sqrt{3} = \tfrac{1}{4}T(1 - \tfrac{1}{2}\sqrt{3})$$

$$S_R V_R = CV_R - \tfrac{1}{2}SC = \tfrac{3}{4}T - \tfrac{1}{2}\,\tfrac{1}{4}T\sqrt{3} = \tfrac{1}{4}T(3 - \tfrac{1}{2}\sqrt{3})$$

$$V_L S_L / S_R V_R = (1 - \tfrac{1}{2}\sqrt{3})/(3 - \tfrac{1}{2}\sqrt{3})$$

$$S_L E = \frac{(A/B)(d_A/w_A)(V_L S_L / S_R V_R)}{[(A/B)(d_A/w_A)(V_L S_L / S_R V_R)] + 1}\,P_{\max}$$

$$= \frac{(A/B)(\sqrt{3})(1 - \tfrac{1}{2}\sqrt{3})/(3 - \tfrac{1}{2}\sqrt{3})}{[(A/B)(\sqrt{3})(1 - \tfrac{1}{2}\sqrt{3})/(3 - \tfrac{1}{2}\sqrt{3})] + 1}\,P_{\max}$$

$$\approx \frac{0.11A}{0.11A + B}\,P_{\max}$$

Note: The complete $S_L E$ formula, as developed on page 154, has to be employed in the P_H projection because $V_L S_L$ and $S_R V_R$ have to be scaled off.

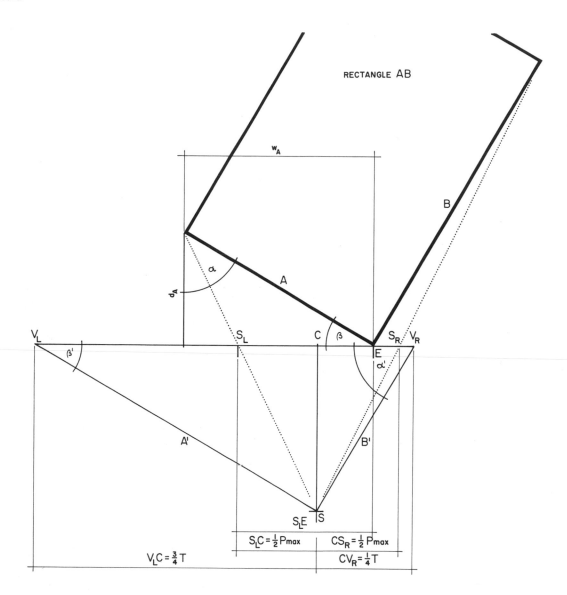

RECTANGLE AB

Fig. 19

$\alpha + \beta = 90° \qquad \alpha = 60° \qquad \beta = 30° \qquad \alpha = \alpha' \qquad \beta = \beta'$

$V_LC = \frac{3}{4}T \qquad CV_R = \frac{1}{4}T \qquad SC = \sqrt{V_LC \times CV_R} = \frac{1}{4}T\sqrt{3}$

$A' = \frac{1}{2}T\sqrt{3} \qquad B' = \frac{1}{2}T \qquad B'/A' = SC/V_LC = d_A/w_A$

$$= 1/\sqrt{3}$$

$V_LS_L = V_LC - \frac{1}{2}SC = \frac{3}{4}T - \frac{1}{2}\frac{1}{4}T\sqrt{3} = \frac{1}{4}T(3 - \frac{1}{2}\sqrt{3})$

$V_LS_L/S_RV_R = (3 - \frac{1}{2}\sqrt{3})/(1 - \frac{1}{2}\sqrt{3})$

$S_LE = \dfrac{(A/B)(d_A/w_A)(V_LS_L/S_RV_R)}{[(A/B)(d_A/w_A)(V_LS_L/S_RV_R)] + 1} P_{\max}$

$\quad = \dfrac{(A/B)(1/\sqrt{3})(3 - \frac{1}{2}\sqrt{3})/(1 - \frac{1}{2}\sqrt{3})}{[(A/B)(1/\sqrt{3})(3 - \frac{1}{2}\sqrt{3})/(1 - \frac{1}{2}\sqrt{3})] + 1} P_{\max}$

$\quad \approx \dfrac{9.11A}{9.11A + B} P_{\max}$

Note: The complete S_LE formula, as developed on page 154, has to be employed in the P_H projection because V_LS_L and S_RV_R have to be scaled off.

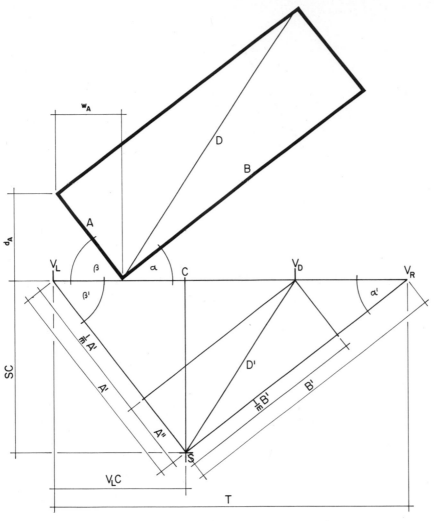

Fig. 20

$$\alpha + \beta = 90° \qquad \alpha' = \alpha \qquad \beta' = \beta$$

$$A \parallel A' \qquad B \parallel B' \qquad D \parallel D' \qquad d_A \parallel SC$$

$$A \perp B \qquad A' \perp B' \qquad d_A \perp T \qquad SC \perp T$$

$$A' - (1/m)A' = A'' \qquad \triangle ABD \sim \triangle A''(1/m)B'D'$$

$$\triangle Ad_Aw_A \sim \triangle A'\,SC\,V_LC \sim \triangle V_LV_D(1/m)B'(1/m)A' \sim \triangle TB'A'$$

$$A'/B' = (1/m)A'/(1/m)B' = V_LC/SC = w_A/d_A$$

$$\frac{A' - (1/m)A'}{(1/m)B'} = \frac{A}{B} \qquad A' = [(A/B)(1/m)(B')] + (1/m)A'$$

$$= \frac{1}{m}\left(\frac{A}{B}B' + A'\right)$$

$$\frac{1}{m} = \frac{A'}{(A/B)B' + A'} \quad \frac{1/B'}{1/B'} = \frac{A'/B'}{A/B + A'/B'} = \frac{V_LC/SC}{A/B + V_LC/SC}$$

$$= \frac{w_A/d_A}{A/B + w_A/d_A}$$

$$V_LV_D = \frac{1}{m}T = \frac{V_LC/SC}{A/B + V_LC/SC}T$$

w_A/d_A can be used, instead of V_LC/SC.

Abbreviated formula for Method 1, 7:

$$\frac{V_LC}{SC} = 2.5$$

therefore

$$V_LV_D = \frac{2.5}{(A/B) + 2.5} V_LV_R$$

The determination of V_LV_D in this method (1, 7) is necessary to determine the depth of the rectangle AB in perspective. Notice that the multiplier in Method 1, 7 is V_LV_R, not T.

V_D—the Vanishing Point of the Diagonal D of the Rectangle AB and Its Determination in the Central Perspective (Re: Method 1, 1)

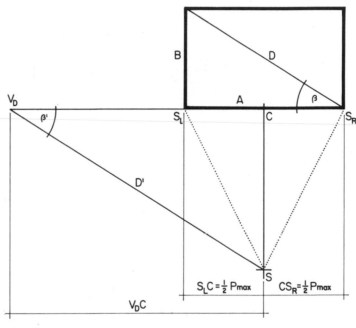

Fig. 21

Side A is part of the picture plane

$B \perp A \qquad SC \perp A \qquad D' \parallel D \qquad D' = SV_D$
$\triangle ABD \sim V_DCS \qquad V_DC/SC = A/B \qquad V_DC = (A/B)SC$

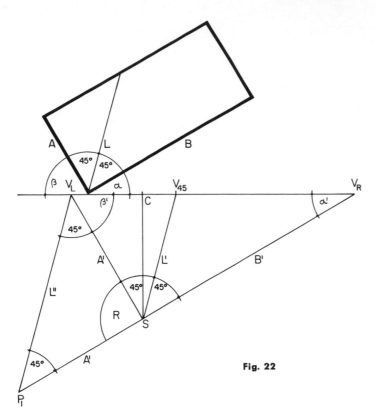

Fig. 22

$$V_L V_R = T \qquad A' \parallel A \qquad B' \parallel B$$
$$L \text{ bisecting } \angle AB \qquad L' \parallel L$$

therefore L' bisects $\angle V_L S V_R$

$$A' \perp A'' \qquad A' \perp B' \qquad A'' = A'$$

therefore

$$L'' \parallel L' \qquad \angle V_L P_1 S = \angle P_1 V_L S = 45°$$

consequently

$$\triangle P_1 V_L V_R \sim \triangle S V_{45} V_R$$
$$\frac{V_L V_{45}}{T} = \frac{A''}{A'' + B'} = \frac{A'}{A' + B'} = \frac{V_L C}{V_L C + SC}$$
$$V_L V_{45} = \frac{V_L C}{V_L C + SC} \, T$$

The purpose and applications of the vanishing point V_{45}, which enables the designer to draw miter lines of squares and rectangular objects easily, are demonstrated in Fig. 23.

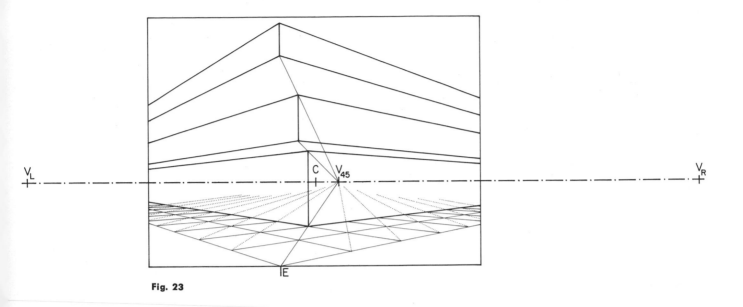

Fig. 23

INDEX